to the Fairhope, AL Library Best wishes Don

THE PRICE OF FREEDOM

The War Within
The Memoir of Don Reeves

SERGEANT DON REEVES
(RETIRED)

Library of Congress Control Number:		2011917514
ISBN:	Hardcover	978-1-4653-7383-0
	Softcover	978-1-4653-7382-3
	Ebook	978-1-4653-7384-7

This book was printed in the United States of America.

To order additional copies of this book, contact:

Xlibris Corporation
1-888-795-4274
www.Xlibris.com
Orders@Xlibris.com
104454

CONTENTS

This book is dedicated to all men and women who fought and died in South Vietnam.

To the South Vietnamese people for the suffering they went through, the loss of their loved ones, and the horrors of war they lived with for over a quarter century.

To all those who worked so hard during that time, at home or on the battlefields to fight against the spread of communism from taking over the world and from taking away our basic right to be free, as God intended us to live, with the right to determine our own destiny.

To the men and women who have worn the uniform of the United States of America to serve their country since the formation of the republic.

To the families that never knew what happened to their loved ones.

To my parents and friends, at home, who worried constantly, not knowing if I was all right.

To my best friend Charlie Hass, who was and still is always there for me.

To my good friends CPL Tommy Nettleton and L/CPL Jimmy Hatfield who gave their lives for me and the rest of the team. Greater love has no man than this, that he gives his life for his friends.

To "The Pretty Lady," my wife Sylvia who never gave up on me, continuously encouraging me through her faith in *God*. Without this precious lady coming into my life, I truly believe I would not be here today. She is the angel *God* sent me.

Most of us take for granted the freedom this country has been blessed with since its inception. But freedom is not free. Many have paid a price in one way or another. Some will never walk again because they have no legs. Some will never hold their children and the ones they love in their arms because they have no arms. Some do not know who they are and wander aimlessly through life desperately searching for a purpose in their life. Some find themselves; many never do. Some have paid with their very lives for freedom.

Regardless of the price, there are others that pay that price with them: parents, perhaps a wife and children, and other loved ones. They too carry some of those scars.

This is my story. The true-to-life experiences of a simple southern boy who, from the age of eleven, always wanted to be a Marine. I found myself in the Vietnam War, at the age of eighteen, that pushed me to the limit and ultimately to the breaking point physically and psychologically. The images I continue to carry in my mind are still horrifying at times, and for many years, I blamed myself for my fallen comrades. Things such as anger, guilt, and bitterness were trapped within my soul and it ate me inside a little every day until there was no more of me left!

Miraculously, I was redeemed when I refound my faith in God and the soul mate who helped me through it all.

PREFACE

I grew up in a small rural town in Saline County, Arkansas, in the late 1940s and 1950s, where at that time bauxite (aluminum ore) was king. Most of my friends' dads worked at Alcoa or Reynolds Metal Company. Working for one of those companies, you were considered well-to-do. If you didn't, you were most likely not doing very well in the financial department, because it was 70 percent of the workforce. My dad was one of the latter; he drove a truck among other jobs.

My dad worked very hard as a truck driver. He worked for Hoskins Trucking in Malvern, Arkansas. When there was work he made good money, but in the fifties we were going through postwar (World War II) recession, and truck driving was good one month and the next month there would not be any freight going out. However, Dad would always find something to fill in when work was slow, though. We always had food on the table and a roof over our head. We moved around a lot, due to my dad's changing jobs frequently, but we always managed to make it back to Bryant.

My mom was a stay-at-home mom like most women in that era, darning socks, patching trousers and shirts, and washing in an old smudge pot outside. I have seen her fingers bleed using a rubboard as she would rub the clothes clean. She cooked all the meals on a wood stove, and everything always turned out just right. It wasn't until 1954 that mom got a washer, gas cook stove, and indoor plumbing, and Dad also bought a television. The antenna was on the outside and you had to turn it toward the strongest part of the signal to receive a good picture. It was crazy how that signal would constantly move.

I was the average all-American boy, though. I had lots of friends. There was Charlie, Richard, Jerry, Mike, Pat, Charles, and JW, to mention a few. You will find throughout this book that I only use first names. When it becomes necessary to use the surnames of these real people, they have been changed in order to protect their privacy, unless prior written and/or verbal permission has been granted.

I did all the average things a boy growing up in Arkansas would do. I would fish in old Mr. Petri's pond, go to the all day movies with Charlie and Richard on Saturdays, and we went to Sunday school and Church and played baseball. Boy, did I play baseball! For two years in a row, we were champs in Babe Ruth, three years in a row district champs, and state champs in 1961. I suppose you know now that baseball was my game and though I don't play anymore, I have never lost my love for it.

Yes, we were poor, even by southern standards. However, I was a happy lad and loved being around my friends and my parents, especially Mama. My daddy was gone most of the time driving a truck, so Mama was not only Mama, but she also filled in for Daddy most of the time, going fishing and tossing the ball around with me when I did not have anyone else to play with. Mama and I had this special relationship. I could confide in her on just about any subject, and she was always there to lend an ear; and when I asked for her advice, it was usually right. When I felt down, she would always encourage me in her own sweet way and tell me everything would be all right. Oh, she was strict and did not mind using the not-so-proverbial peach switch when she and I didn't see eye to eye, which was pretty often in my early years.

I was the average student in school. There was one year in the third grade when my parents moved four times, to three different school districts, which caused me to fail that grade. In the seventh grade, I failed because I got lazy. When I was in the tenth grade, I contracted pneumonia. When I was almost over it, I had a relapse, which set me back that year as well.

I decided to leave school and go to work full-time at Mr. Pickens's dairy farm. I had been working on the farm for about two years, part-time. I loved that job. I loved the cows and especially Dan, the horse I rode to herd the cattle. Dan and I had this special relationship too; I loved him and he knew it. He also returned that love.

In the late 1950s, there was baseball, fishing, hunting, school, church, and rock 'n' roll. Then, I kept hearing in the news about this place called Vietnam. It was a place that seemed so far away and they said that those people had been fighting over there for over twenty years. I didn't think much about it because it was so far away from Arkansas, and it did not matter much to me. Why would a fourteen-year-old boy in Arkansas want to know about a place halfway around the world anyway? However, four years later, I not only found out where Vietnam was, but I also found myself right smack dab in the middle of someone else's war.

CHAPTER ONE

The Early Years

Growing Up

Growing up as an only child, living in Arkansas, the 1950s were interesting, to say the least. In the summer of 1951, we lived with my grandparents in Benton, Arkansas. I was five years old. For my fifth birthday, I got a brand-new Western Flyer tricycle. Mama would only let me ride it in the yard, but I would imagine that I was a truck driver like Daddy, and I got real good at dodging the holes and the ruts in the yard. I had a great time pretending!

There was a neighbor kid from the block over who decided he wanted my tricycle, so he came in my yard and told me, "I'm going to beat you up if you don't give me your tricycle." I told him that I would beat him up if he tried. Well, he did *try,* and we were on . . . I had him down and was hitting him with all I had, and he was yelling and crying! My mama heard all the commotion and came out to see what was going on. She pulled me off him and asked me what started all this. I told her that he started it because he tried to take my tricycle away from me. Mama explained to the boy that it was not his to take, but asked us if we could take turns playing with it, because the two of us would have a much better time. Then she added that we need to be friends and be good to each other. She made both of us apologize. Well, that boy's name was Charlie. Charlie and I became very good friends. It is a friendship that has stood the test of time to this day (sixty years at this writing). Charlie introduced me to his best friend Richard, and it wasn't long before the three of us were inseparable. We would play in Richard's chicken yard from early morning to early night, pretending that we were soldiers and we would chase the enemy. One day we were fighting the Japanese, the next day the Germans, day in and day out, during the summer. The chickens were the Japanese and Germans, and of course we would always win!

On Saturday we called a ceasefire on the chickens in order to go to the movies in downtown Benton. It was a long walk from Owasso Hill in Benton to go downtown. Charlie and I would receive a weekly allowance of twenty-five cents. Richard would only get his twenty-five cents allowance once a month. Richard lived with his grandmother, who was very poor and could not afford to give him money every week (money was real tight in the south back then). In order for the three of us to attend the show, we would pool our money. All three of us would be down at the Benton Courier newspaper office early on Saturday morning. We had to be early because most of the other kids were doing the same thing, and we wanted to get the best corners in town and also be the first out there to sell our papers. We would buy ten papers and the three of us would sell them for ten cents. We doubled our money! *Wow*! The three of us would go to the movie, buy popcorn, candy, and cokes, all from the dollar we made. In those days it only cost ten cents to get in to see the movie. We would stay there until dark, watching the show over and over until the theatre manager would run us out of the place. We had the best of times, but realized it wasn't as much fun unless the three of us were together.

In August that year, Mama and Daddy moved to Bauxite. It was only six miles from Benton, but to me it seemed like it was clear across the state of Arkansas. Mama and Daddy told me I could go to my grandparents on Friday nights and stay the weekend, so I could play with Charlie and Richard. This turned out to be hard to do because we didn't have a car. I would have to get my uncle Charles to come and get me to take me to Grandpa's house. If, for some reason, my uncle Charles could not take me, then I would walk to Benton. I just couldn't wait to get there! The closer I got, the faster I would walk until I would be running. I could not wait to see my friends. When I would finally arrive, Richard would say, "What took you so long?"

My first day at school was a huge challenge. I did not know anyone because we had just moved to Bauxite and I didn't have time yet to make friends. My first grade teacher was Ms. Fitzhugh. She was very nice to me; however, I did not want to be there! I was real scared of everyone, and I had never been away from my parents or grandparents in my entire life. I was dropped off at an unfamiliar place, and I felt abandoned and alone. The teacher contacted Mama, and she came and took me home and gave me a lecture about how important school was and that I needed a good solid education, and, besides, she said, "It's the law that you go to school." Day two, the same thing happened. When Mama came to the school *this* time, she had the peach tree switch. She grabbed me up out of my desk and said, "Young man, I did not come to take you home. I came to give you a spanking." She lit into me like there was no tomorrow, right in front of the entire class! Then she walked me back to my seat, kissed me on the cheek, and said, "I will see you when school is out. I love you." From that day forward, I *liked school*!

In the winter of 1954, my daddy was laid off his job. He looked everywhere for another, but to no avail. Daddy had a cousin who lived in Rockford, Illinois. In the spring of 1955, Daddy told us he was going up there to look for work, and that as soon as he got settled, he would send us money so we could join him. We had to move back to Grandpa's. That wasn't all bad, though, because I would be close to Charlie and Richard. Later, I realized how much I missed my daddy.

The day *finally* came when money arrived in the mail for us to leave and go to Rockford. We said our goodbyes and climbed aboard the Continental Trailways bus. This was exciting because I had never ridden on a bus. Seeing the sites and countryside was exciting the first day, but by the second day I started asking, "Are we there yet? When are we going to get there?" About the middle of the third day, we finally arrived, and Daddy was there to meet us. I sure was glad to see him! He rented a trailer, and it was a lot nicer than most anything we had ever lived in, although it was old, small, and needed work. Jess, my daddy's cousin, loved to drink beer and watch baseball on TV. This is when I really started to get serious about baseball and wanting to play the game.

I was entering into the fourth grade in school, and I had a long walk to Morris Kennedy Elementary. Every day I made that walk to school, it seemed to be colder each time. It wasn't like Arkansas, where a light coat in November was enough. It was already snowing and bitterly cold.

When it started snowing, I never saw dirt again until late April. Mama had been trying to get Daddy to pack up and move back to Bryant, but Daddy kept on saying, "I have a good job and we are doing okay, and there is nothing back in Arkansas for us." This subject came up a lot. Mama was not happy in Rockford and I wasn't either. I think Daddy felt the same, but looking back, I believe Daddy knew that staying was the right thing to do for his family financially.

It was the middle of April and snowing. Mama told Daddy, "If it snows in the month of May, Don and I are leaving and going back home to Arkansas."

Daddy laughed and said, "If it does snow in the month of May, I will pack up and go with you, but that will not happen." Guess what! It did happen. It snowed eight inches on May first! So we packed up and left Rockford, Illinois. Although it meant doing without good clothes, a nice place to stay, I was glad to be going home.

My Grandfather

Nicholi Patrikavich was born in 1889, in what used to be known as the Austro-Hungarian Empire. In late 1904, trouble erupted in that country between the Slovaks and the Russians. As things heated up politically, it was imminent war was on the horizon. The citizens of that country were beginning to be in harm's way. This was the beginning of the Bolshevik Revolution. The Bolsheviks marched against the Slovaks and the Empire, destroying it and the people who resisted them.

According to my mother, the following is an account of how my grandfather survived and made his way to America and the life he led after arriving in the United States.

Two years after the invasion, my great grandparents and their two sons would hide in any place they could, along with others. They would go from place to place, usually underground in tunnels, in friend's homes, in attics, anywhere it was safe. As the Russians would find the hiding places, one by one, my great grandparents would seek out another, sometimes only narrowly escaping. When they ran out of places to hide, my great grandparents decided to leave the country and try to go to America. During this attempt, they found out that everyone wanted money, which was something they did not have, because the revolution had torn down the country's infrastructure. They would have to try and smuggle aboard a ship and take their chances. It was obvious to them that all four would not be able to do this.

My great grandparents made the decision to allow the boys to smuggle aboard without them and they would try to go later. My grandfather and his brother didn't want to go without their parents, but knew that in order to save their lives, it was the only way. My great uncle was seventeen and my grandfather was only fifteen at the time. They travelled at night and hid out during the daylight hours trying to make it to the coast. They traveled for over a month, living off the land and whatever they could find, without being detected. They found a French freighter leaving for the United States, and they smuggled aboard and hid out in one of the holds. After four days and nights without food and only a small container of water they had brought on board (which had been depleted the day before), they knew they had to take their chances and leave the hold and try to find food and water. When they reached topside of the ship, they were detected and taken to the ship's captain. As it turned out, the captain had run across this situation before. He was lenient and decided to allow them to work for their passage as deckhands.

After three weeks of very rough seas in the North Atlantic, they arrived at New York Harbor and disembarked from the vessel. My grandfather and his brother were taken to Ellis Island, where they started the procedure for legalization in the United States. After this process, they were given a change of clothes and five dollars. If an immigrant wished, he could legally change his name. My grandfather and great uncle decided to do so. From then on, Grandpa was known as Nick Patrick, and my great uncle took the name John Patrick. Grandpa and Uncle John never heard from their parents again. It is believed that they were probably killed or perhaps died of exposure. They sacrificed their lives so that their children could begin a new life in America.

Grandpa and Uncle John left New York and found their way to Pittsburgh, PA. They both found work in the steel mill there. Grandpa worked at the mill for three years and decided to head west to see some of the country. Working his way across the country, doing anything that was available, he learned several trades. He worked as a blacksmith, farmhand, cattle driver, and barber. He also worked in the copper mines in Colorado and other places as well. He wandered around, seeing different parts of the country for another five years before settling in Arkansas. He lost track of Uncle John around 1915. Many were the times he tried to find him but to no avail. He never heard from his brother again.

My Grandpa met Grandma (Alice Gretta) in 1917, and they were married. They moved to Chicot County, where they tried sharecropping for two or three years, until the bottom fell out of the market. Grandpa heard that in Saline County, the Aluminum Company of America (ALCOA) was building a plant to manufacture bauxite (aluminum ore) into aluminum. They decided to pack up their belongings and make the trip to Central Arkansas. Their transportation consisted of a horse and wagon; it was tough and very slow, taking about two weeks to complete the trip.

When they arrived in Saline County, ALCOA hired Grandpa on the spot because of his experience in the steel mills. The town of Bauxite was a company town owned by ALCOA. ALCOA built houses, a movie theater, schools, stores, gas stations, all at the company's expense. They didn't have much problem finding a place to live because Grandpa and Grandma would live in one of the company's houses for the next thirty years. When ALCOA decided to dismantle the town and turn it into an open pit mine, my grandparents moved to Benton. This was after the federal government declared that it was illegal for a company to own or monopolize a town or community.

My grandpa had some special gifts. I believe *God* gave them to him. Maybe it was the reason he and his brother were able to escape to America.

One of those gifts was the ability to tell fortunes with regular playing cards. Grandpa and Grandma had ten children. He told nine of his children their fortune, and their life turned out exactly the way he told it. Everything was true, down to the color of the hair, eyes, and financial status of the people they married. He told my Uncle Sam that he would marry seven times and it happened! He told my mother she would care for two men. One was well-to-do and would have red hair. The other would be blackheaded and poor. He went on to say that she would marry the poor man. He told this to her when she was only twelve. Later in her life, Mama asked Grandpa, "How did you know this?"

He replied, "Because you have a kind heart and I knew you would choose a man with a kind heart also."

"But how did you know Avery (my dad) would be the one with the kind heart?" she asked.

He replied, "Because it was in the cards." He would not tell my Aunt Ruth's fortune though. My mama said she asked him many times to tell her fortune, but he would smile and say, "You have no fortune." My aunt Ruth died of leukemia, at the age of thirty-two.

He also had the ability to see visions of things to come and dreams that he was able to interpret correctly. After my first overseas tour and stint in Vietnam, I came home on leave to visit with my grandpa. (Grandma passed away in 1961.) While visiting with him, I told him, "Grandpa, I have a thirty-day leave, and I am going to spend most of them with you."

My grandpa said to me, "No, you not have but nine or ten days here. You will go back and fight. You will be a brave warrior. You will save many lives and be honored. You will be hurt and get sick but you will be okay."

"No, Grandpa, I have already served my time overseas. I don't have to go back for two or three years. I do not have to be on the train back to California for another twenty-eight days."

My grandpa had a very worried look on his face, and he said, "You no take train. Take bus. Train will be sure death for you. No take train." Then he said something that cut me to the core. "When you get back, I not be here."

"Where are you going, Grandpa?" I asked.

"I go home to be with Grandma," he said. I did not want to believe any of this and was being cautiously optimistic that none of this would happen.

I had been home on leave for nine days when I got the call from my unit at Camp Pendleton that all leaves had been canceled and that I was to report back to base immediately within five days. I had to leave on the first bus bound for California in order to make it back to camp in time. No, I did not take the train. I had a layover in El Paso, Texas, waiting for my connection. When I walked in the terminal, crowds of people were standing by several televisions inside the building. The *special news report* was talking about a passenger train that had derailed thirty-five miles east of El Paso. There were few survivors. I had to sit down because I was about to faint. How did my grandfather know? Was it a guess? Was it coincidence? I don't think so. I believe that the vision he saw was real. I believe it was from God, because it was 100 percent accurate. He was also right when he said that he would not be here when I returned home.

My grandfather was a huge influence in my life, and he continues to be an inspiration to me. Some of his favorite things he said to me were things like these: "A penny saved is a penny earned. A rolling stone collects no moss. Treat people the way you want to be treated, even the people who don't like you. Strangers are only friends we haven't met. Always keep your word. Admit your mistakes. Don't lie, cheat, or steal. Never leave a task undone. Give a man an honest day's work, and he will give you an honest wage. Always look for the good in others; and remember you have *your* bad side too. Be of good cheer. Treat your spouse with respect and love her with all your heart because the two of you are as one. Isn't that what you want? Love God." All of these statements we have heard a thousand times over, but this was a man who lived by every one of them.

My Mother

My mother was the best but what child doesn't believe that about his mother. When I was four, we lived on Asher Avenue, a main artery and very busy street in Little Rock, Arkansas. Only a short walk to where Daddy worked. Daddy drove a truck for East Texas Motor Freight Lines and he was gone three to four days at a time. Mama was always trying to keep me occupied by playing with me. We would sit down on the floor and roll a ball back and forth, and she tried to teach me how to play jacks (a girl's game), but I couldn't get interested in it. She would stand the dominoes up all in a roll and then have me knock 'em down, and I would have the time of my life watching them fall! She taught me how to play marbles (a game kind of like pool, only you play it on the ground). She would draw a circle in the dirt; then she would place all these marbles in the circle, give me one marble, show me how to hold it, and tell me to knock the marbles out of the circle. When I couldn't do it I would get mad and cry, and she would hug me, tell me not to cry, and keep trying until I got the hang of it (that is what she would do when she would see me unhappy). After a couple of days, I did get the hang of it! I would challenge Mama to a game of marbles, and Mama would usually say yes. As long as you are hitting marbles out of the circle you get to keep shooting, but when you miss, it's the other person's turn, but I didn't want to let her have a turn. I would always want to shoot over again, but she wouldn't let me. She was always teaching me about how to play fair.

There was this little creek about a block from where we lived, where Mama would take me fishing. There weren't any fish in the creek, but I did not know it at the time. She would get a short stick and tie some string on the end of it, and on the other end she would shape one of her bobby pins in the form of a fish hook, throw it in the water, tell me to be real still and quiet, and that I might catch a fish; the *key* word here is *might*! I would wait for what I thought was an hour but was only a minute or two and no fish. We would try another place, then another. I would tell Mama that the fish were not biting, so we would grab the pole, go get ice cream, and eat it on the way home. I liked going fishing because every time we left the creek, I knew that Mama would buy ice cream!

I remember all my friends loved Mama. She always treated them like her own, scolded them when they were wrong, and praised them when they were right. When we would come in from school, my friends knew that Mama would have donuts! Jerry, Mike, and Charles would beat me home from school, and sneak donuts when Mama wasn't looking, and leave me without any. If she caught them, she would run them out of the house with a switch. They got a big kick out of it; they knew Mama wouldn't hurt them even if her life depended on it. My home was always their home away from home.

Mama would help me with my school homework. She would sit up until early hours in the morning making sure I understood what I needed to know, even thought this was after putting in a full day of keeping house, washing, ironing, and cooking. She never seemed to mind.

Mama was always in church on Sunday, and she insisted I was there too. Her faith in God never failed. When things were not going so well, she would always say, "As long as we do what is right, do the best we can, God will provide" . . . and she was right, because He always did. One particular time, when I was fifteen, Daddy was out of work and no one was hiring. Mama would make breakfast, lunch, and dinner with only flour and water. She would make water gravy and biscuits because flour was all we could afford. We ate that for six weeks. She was right . . . God did provide because she did the best she could and did the right thing and never complained about the hardship. When I left for the service, her last words to me as I left to board the plane were, "Always do the right thing, do your best, and always trust in God, and He will see you through." She always wanted me to be dedicated to the tasks at hand. She told me when I was twelve, "Once a task is begun, never leave it till it's done, be it large or be it small, do it well or not at all." I have never forgotten those words, though I have been guilty of sometime not completing something I started, and those words will come back to haunt me until I finish it.

She was at every ball game and every function at school, rooting me on. She even made Daddy move to California when I went into the service. I didn't like that too much, but later on I did, because it gave me some place to go. Mama was this special person that was always there when you needed her. I always felt safe when I was with her, and as I look back on my childhood, they were the greatest and most wonderful years of my life, and I owe that to my Mama. It broke my heart when she passed away (2009). I know without a doubt that her spirit is still with me because, when I am alone, or thinking back of my childhood, or have her on my mind, or am concerned about something, I can feel her sweet spirit caressing me; and again, I feel safe . . . and I look up toward the heavens and say, "Thanks, Mom."

My Dad

Daddy drove a truck most of his working life, so I didn't see much of him in the early years. As a matter of fact, when I was four years old, I thought the word daddy was a word that my Mama used when she couldn't think of anything else to say! When I did see him though during that time, he was always telling me what a big boy I was and asked me if I had been good. When I was five, I knew who Daddy was, and tried to imitate him on my tricycle by pretending I was driving a big truck like him. Through my eyes, he was this gigantic figure of a man that could do anything, though he was only five feet eight inches tall.

Daddy always sounded like this strict disciplinarian who never carried out his threats; he would just keep on shouting at the top of his lungs not to do this or not to do that. In the early years, he had me so confused; I did not know what was right or what was wrong. At the age of six, Daddy bought me a baseball glove, ball, and bat, and when he was home he would teach me to catch and hit the ball. I got bold of it after about the fifth or sixth time we played and I told Daddy to throw the ball up high, like a fly ball. He did not want to because he didn't think I was ready for that. I said I was, so reluctantly he did. That ball hit me exactly in the forehead. I was crying and carrying on like I was going to die! He came running over to me like it was my last day on earth and said, "Don, are you all right, son"; and I would cry that much harder. After he looked me over and saw I was okay, he said, "I told you that you were not ready for a fly ball! Maybe next time you will listen to me!" I said, "I don't want to play ever again!" Of course, that statement was false. A couple of days later, I decided that in order to get ready to catch fly balls, I would have to throw the ball up in the air myself and try to catch it. It took me awhile, but I was doing pretty well by the next time Daddy came home. I showed him what I could do and he said that it was good. Then he started mixing up the pitches that he threw to me. He taught me the fundamentals of baseball, and I got pretty good at it. We played every chance we got; that is, until I was about eight and a half, then he would say he did not have time. When I was nine, Daddy had been laid off work permanently because of the recession, and he was out of work. I saw Daddy cry for the first time in my life. When I asked Mama what was wrong, she told me that Daddy was worried about finding a job because there were not any around. At the age of nine, I don't believe I fully understood what she said, but I knew that it meant we were in trouble because Mama was putting stuff in boxes, and about a week later we were back at Grandpa and Grandma's house, and Daddy had left and did not tell me where he was going and I cried my eyes out. Mama told me that he had to go to Illinois to look for a job and that things would be all right soon.

At the age of twelve, we were back in Arkansas, and I was playing Little League. Daddy still drove a truck, but was home most nights, so he got to come to most of my games. I would hear him rooting me on above everyone else. When the game was over, he would critique my performance . . . with all negatives. He made me feel like I was the worst player on the field; and I felt like I was about two feet tall after he finished telling me how bad I was. He never mentioned the hits I got or the great catches I made: to him, it was all about the mistakes! The more I tried to please him, the worse I would get; he said, I was like a monkey in a barrel trying to get out, and too dumb to do it! I got so discouraged I didn't want to play anymore, and if it had not been for Mama encouraging me, I probably would have quit. It wasn't just baseball; it was everything I tried to do! I got so tired of feeling like a loser and I thought about running away from home; or maybe I would get this terminal illness (like the kid in "A Christmas Story" imagined); then I would get all this attention, and he would cry, saying he was sorry, and he would never say bad things to me again. Yeah . . . right! I was afraid to talk to Daddy after that year, for fear he would whip me or twist things around, so I talked with Mama about how I felt. She told me that when Daddy pointed out the mistakes and why I made them, he just wanted me to correct them. I don't think she really believed what she was telling me, because a couple of days later, I came home from playing with my friends, and Mama and Daddy were arguing about me. After that, Daddy toned down . . . quite a bit.

The best years of my childhood with Daddy were the next three years, when he took on the assistant managing chores with my Babe Ruth baseball team.

Dad had his good side too; like the time when I was at the local independent grocery store when I was thirteen, buying a coke and a bag of chips; the owner, Mr. Marshall, said, "There is talk going around, son, that you are a pretty good ball player." I asked him where he heard that, and he told me, "From your Dad." I said, "Really!" He told me yes and then added, "Your dad is real proud of you, Don . . . keep up the good work, we need that championship, okay?" I assured him that I would and left the store; I was on cloud nine, and from then on, I did not let anything bother me for a long time. When I was fourteen, times got hard again and it was the Christmas season (it was the time when all my parents could afford to buy to eat was flour. Dad asked me what I wanted for Christmas, and I told him that I did not want or need anything this Christmas because I knew we were having a hard time and Christmas was the last thing on my mind. However, I had been looking at a little box camera at the same local grocery store. I never told Mom or Dad about that camera I wanted so bad, but when Dad and I would go to the store to get flour, I would go to the shelf where it was to see if it was still there; oh, it was a beautiful blue 620 box camera, and it was something I had been wanting for a long time. I would go in everyday looking to see if it was still there, for when things got better, thinking that maybe I could buy it when I started getting my allowance again. One day (Dec. 23 to be exact), I went in to check on the camera like I normally did, and I didn't see it! My heart went into my throat; I couldn't swallow; I was so heartbroken! Someone had bought my camera! I cried most of the way home. I say most of the way but it was actually all the way home! I kept walking down the street, because I didn't want Mom or Dad to see me crying, so I walked around until I stopped crying and went home. Mom asked me where I had been; I told her, just walking around. Mom sensed my depression about Christmas, and she and Dad told me they were sorry that Christmas wasn't happening this year; Mom was crying, which made me cry again. Well, that was the second time I saw him cry. I assured both of them that it wasn't things that were important at Christmas but the love we have for each other, and the three of us were the richest people in town because we have more love for each other than anyone else! And I meant every word of it! I realized something that day. I grew up a little more. I realized that

Christmas was the celebration of our Lord's birthday. It is a day set aside to remind us that we are supposed to have this spirit with us everyday. It is through the hardest of times that we receive our greatest blessings and realize the wonderful love that is always with us, that sometimes we take for granted.

Christmas Day came, and to everyone's surprise, when we opened the door to feed the dog, there was this beautiful blue box camera, between the screen and the wood door! No one knew where it came from! If Mom and Dad knew, they took it to their grave. I asked them several times after I was an adult, and they both said they did not know. They said, when they asked Mr. Marshall about it, he said that he sold it, but the person wanted to remain anonymous. So we never knew who brought it. Could it have been a stranger, or maybe an angel, or maybe, thinking back though, I think it might have been Mr. Marshall. Maybe there really is a Santa Claus, after all!

My relationship with my dad was much better throughout the rest of my time at home. We had a great relationship and we were close for years, until another hard bump in the road many years later (but that is for a later chapter). I lost my dad in 1994, twelve days after my parents' fiftieth wedding anniversary, and his funeral was held two days before my birthday. I think about him every day; and when I make a little dumb mistake, I can hear him say, "Don, you're just like a monkey in a barrel trying to get out, and too dumb to do it!" And I smile, because I know, he loves me.

The Teen Years

Spring of 1959 was turning out to be promising in the good times department. School was almost out for the summer and baseball practice was in full swing. My age had graduated me to Babe Ruth League status and it was so exciting to play like the big boys. Dad had an accident on his truck, hurting his leg. He took a job working as a mechanic at a Little Rock car dealership and was home every night. I enjoyed him being home. He would be able to come to my games. He even volunteered to be one of the assistant coaches.

Our manager, Mr. Otis Hall, made Dad the infield coach. I was really surprised at how much Dad knew about baseball. He and Mr. Hall really had us looking sharp. This would be the first year for Babe Ruth baseball in Bryant, and all the community was turning out for our games. I suppose they kept coming back because we kept winning.

There were eight teams in our league: four teams in the south district, which was Benton; two teams from Benton, one from Traskwood community and one from Harmony Grove, made up the south district. The north district consisted of two teams from Bryant, one from Bauxite and one from Sardis community. I played on one of the Bryant teams, named after the sponsor, Fletcher's Insurance.

Half way through the season, we were in first place, losing only one game to Roland's Grocery, the other Bryant team. Our next game was with Sardis community. Their ace pitcher was Dillard Wayne. Dillard was a good pitcher with good control as long as he didn't get rattled. He was known for his fast curve ball that broke down and out to a right-handed hitter. When Dillard would get rattled, the pitcher's mound became a personal vendetta. To him, it wasn't a game anymore; it was a way to get even. He would start throwing for the head instead of the plate. I had warned him earlier in the season (after he hit me on purpose) that if he did it again, I was coming after him. He had no reply. I was up to bat my third time going for my third hit. I crowded the plate, challenging him to hit me. He took his stretch and let it fly. Dillard barely missed me on the first pitch. He only meant to brush me off the plate. The next pitch was a ball as well. The next pitch was a taken strike. The next three pitches I fouled off, one of them over the left field fence. It's what he did next that I will never forget. If looks could kill, I was dead that day! When I got back into the batter's box, Dillard pointed at me and said, "You are going down." I walked about halfway to the mound and said, "If you hit me on purpose, you are going down; that is my last warning to you." I walked back to the plate, took a couple of practice swings and reentered the batter's box. Dillard wasn't looking at his catcher. He was looking at me. Then he took his stretch and threw the ball. It was coming right for my head! I did not move. I scrunched my shoulder to cover myself. The ball hit me in the helmet, and as promised, I went after him. Then both teams joined in out on the field and the fight was on. I believe it took over thirty minutes to restore order on the field. Dillard and I were out of the game and told to leave the field. The Bryant city constable, Rufus Berry, escorted us off the field separately. When Dad came home, he said that there were also several spectators who started fighting. They were asked to leave as well, and the game was called. Even though Fletcher's Insurance was ahead and five full innings were played, the league council made us replay the game at the end of the regular season. It turned out that we did not have to play that game over, because even if we had lost the game we still would have won the league championship outright. So we took the forfeit.

The following year we also won the league championship, and the year after that. We went to the Arkansas state championship. Fletcher's Insurance had managed to make it to the finals in the tournament! The other team in the finals was Coleman Dairy, a team from the Little Rock Metro league. Coleman Dairy had won state three years in a row. Earlier in the tournament, we defeated Coleman Dairy and put them in the losers bracket, and in order for Coleman Dairy to win the tournament, they had to beat us twice. We only had to beat them once to win state since they had a previous loss. Charles Road was pitching for us and I was playing shortstop. Charles was our ace, a southpaw who had a mean slider and a monster fast ball that had been clocked at over ninety MPH. For Coleman Dairy, the pitcher was Randy Griffin. He was a great right-hander with a mean *everything*! They called him "The Iron Man." In Babe Ruth baseball, seven innings is a regulation game. We were in the eleventh inning. We did not get a hit off the iron man at all, only infield grounders, that resulted in outs; "The Iron Man" was going for the perfect game. Charles was equally as good that night. He had only given up one hit and one walk. With two outs in the bottom of the eleventh inning, Corky Chennault was at bat for Fletcher's Insurance. The first pitch was a ball and the second as well. The next two pitches were strikes which Corky fouled off. The count was two and two. The next pitch was a fast ball right down the middle. "The Iron Man" finally made a mistake! You did not throw Corky a fast ball down the middle and not pay for it! He swung and gave it a ride. Going, going, going, gone . . . home run! It was the one and only hit we were able to muster against Randy, but it proved to be enough. We had won the Arkansas State Championship, 1 to 0. I failed to mention one thing. Randy, "Iron Man" Griffin was out of innings after the sixth. Babe Ruth regulations only permitted a pitcher to pitch thirteen innings in a seven-day period. We just knew we had the game won after the sixth inning, but Randy came out in the seventh wearing a glove on his right hand! Mr. Hall and Dad protested. The umpire searched the rules on this situation and came up with no solution. The rule book stated that a pitcher must rest the pitching arm for a minimum of six days after he has pitched a maximum of thirteen innings. The rule book only said to rest the *arm* not the person! It was determined that Randy could pitch with his left arm. He was equally as good with his left as he was with his right. We all found out that night why they called him, "The Iron Man."

Life wasn't all about baseball, though. There was school, girls, rock 'n' roll, girls, hunting, fishing, girls, and of course work. I worked for Mr. Pickens who owned a dairy farm about two miles south of Bryant. When I was almost fifteen, I would visit with Patricia (Pat), Mr. Pickens's daughter. She had chores on the farm too and I would walk around the farm helping her get her work done. It was also the only time we had to talk. After about two months of that, Mr. Pickens said, "Hell, boy, you might as well go on the payroll. You spend more time here than you do at home." Pat and I were good friends, not sweet on each other, just good friends. She taught me to ride a horse, and that is where I met Dan. He was a beautiful chestnut with a white face, a very gentle cow pony, who really knew what he was doing when it came to cows. When I rode Dan, I would talk to him and carry on a conversation with him and sometime, I swear, he knew what I was saying. It got to the point that Dan would not let anyone else ride him unless I told him it was okay, then he would settle down. It was if he did not want to hurt my feelings by allowing someone else on his back. For some reason, ever since I can remember, I have always had a special bond with animals and they have bonded with me. Mama said I missed my calling by not becoming a veterinarian.

My responsibilities at the dairy started at four-thirty in the morning. When I woke up, I would get ready for school, and ride my bike to the farm, saddle up Dan, and we would herd the cows into the milking barn. When I was done, it was time to eat breakfast. Ms. Pickens and Pat would have breakfast ready and it was always *so* good, ham and eggs, orange juice and milk. When it was time to leave for school, Pat would give me a ride in her car. When school was out for the day, it was back to the dairy, cleaning the stalls in the milking barn and making sure the cows had plenty of water, grain, and hay in the big barn. At six-thirty or when I got done, it was home to do my school homework, then an hour or so of TV and to bed. Sounds like a dull life, huh? On the contrary, it was one of the most enjoyable experiences I have ever had. Mr. and Ms. Pickens were almost like second parents and Pat took the place of the sister I never had. I made six dollars a day, thirty dollars a week and sometimes a bonus for working over. In the early summer and fall was hay cutting on the farm. Mr. Pickens put me in charge of getting it put up into the hay barns. He would pay me thirty cents per bale. I hired my friends Jerry Hall and Charles Blalock to help. Out of my thirty cents, I paid them eight cents a bale. In the summer cut, we would put up around four to five thousand bales of hay, and in the fall cut around, two to three thousand. The first year I worked on the farm, counting the hauling of hay, I made one thousand nine hundred dollars. I helped with the finances at home and bought a 1952 Ford pickup. Man, was it sharp! I believe to date it is the only vehicle I paid cash for! It had a flathead V-8 motor with a three speed on the column. I later had it painted a midnight blue and put flipper wheels and dual smokestacks going up behind the cab. I was the talk of the town for a while, until Mac Magill's father bought him a 1957 Studebaker Silver Hawk. It was okay, though. Everyone knew his dad financed that Studebaker and all my friends knew about it. I was the only sixteen-year-old with a truck that I paid for with my own money. Three months later, Mac wrecked his Silver Hawk, totaling it out. In the process, Mac was hurt really badly. He lost an eye and his left leg. Our neighborhood was never quite the same without seeing Mac and his Studebaker.

Saturday nights was like any other small town in the south. If there were sidewalks in Bryant, Arkansas, they would have rolled up at dusk. We had to go to Benton or Little Rock for excitement. Being under the age of seventeen, we only had learners' permits and that meant you had to have a licensed driver in the vehicle with you, so Little Rock was out. We all resorted to plan "B," which was to go to Benton, the county seat. Well, it was really plan "A" because our parents would not let us go to Little Rock on Saturday anyway.

All the cops in Benton knew this but they didn't bother us, unless someone was showing off or drinking. If we were showing off, they called our parents and we got what for and were grounded for an eternity. Anyone caught drinking was the kiss of death. You have heard the statement "one bad apple spoils the whole barrel!" When a kid from Bryant was caught drinking while driving, he got a ride to the Benton police station, courtesy of the taxpayers. The kid's parents were called, and they paid a fine and took their misguided child home. After that, the police cracked down on all of the innocent bystanders, stopping us for *anything* and then making us leave Benton at nine o'clock. This would go on for several weeks until we won their trust back.

The Benton drive inn theater was a place to meet people of the opposite sex and just to have fun and watch a good movie. There wasn't any cable or satellite TV back then, so a trip to the drive inn was a real treat for most of us. On Saturday night you could get into the drive inn theater for only fifty cents per car, up to four people. All over four had to pay fifty cents each. Dad let me have the family car on this particular night. There were five of us: myself, Jerry, Charles Blalock, Don, and Ronnie Gwen. Ronnie was the smallest, so we decided to put him into the trunk of the car until we parked inside the theatre. Everyone was excited to see the movie and see who else was there. We decided to get out of the car and sit up by the concession area to watch the movie. We were having a good time watching the show, and we had hooked up with some girls trying to impress them when it hit me like a ton of bricks (about forty minutes after we arrived) that we had left little Ronnie in the trunk! We all just knew he was dead! If he wasn't, we were going to have a crybaby on our hands and that was going to spoil our chances of picking up any girls. When we arrived at the car and opened the trunk, there Ronnie was curled up like a fetus in a womb, bawling his eyes out and weak from banging on the trunk and shouting at the top of his lungs. We helped him out, apologizing over and over, but it didn't do any good. He said he would forgive us and not tell his or our parents of the incident if we would buy all of his popcorn, cokes, and I don't know what all for the next three days. Like dummies we all said, "Okay, we will do it." By noon on Monday, the entire city of Bryant knew about what happened, but payback was h-e-l-l! He did keep his promise, though. He told the whole city of Bryant but he did not tell his or our parents. They found out through the grapevine. Not only did we get what for but also, later, everyone had a big laugh!

In the late summer of 1961, my parents moved back to Malvern, Arkansas, which was forty miles southwest of Bryant. Dad had gone into the pulpwood business. He bought a truck and two horses. That meant leaving my job at the dairy farm and all my friends. I was familiar with Malvern because we lived there when I was in the third grade. I was hoping to hook up with my old friends there by turning a bad situation into a good one. I renewed my acquaintances with most of them: Tommy Cost, Phil and David Clemmons, David and Wayne Hopkins, and there was *Pauletta*. I thought she was the prettiest girl I had ever seen. We were sweet on each other and she loved to go to church. She would come to my house on Sunday morning and we would walk to the First Assembly of God Church on Main Street for Sunday school and the main service. We would walk back to my house where she would eat lunch with us and I would walk her home. That was the extent of our relationship; however, I think we both wanted it to be more but were too shy to take it any farther.

Most of my time at Malvern was taken up with school and helping Dad in the log woods. However, things were not going very well with the pulpwood business. Dad had this really great knack for venturing into something when there was a down market economically. By the fall of 1962, things were getting real bad and Dad decided to cut his losses and go back to driving a truck. It meant selling the horses, and letting the truck and equipment go back to the creditor, and pay off the help. Our last trip to the woods was Thanksgiving of 1962, and a very cold drizzle, which turned to sleet later in the day. I started running a fever, and Dad told me to get into the truck where it was warm. Dad and my half-brothers, Jim and Earl, continued to load the truck. When they loaded all they could, due to the weather, I was so sick I was near convulsions. When we got home, Dad had to carry me into the house because I was so weak with fever. Doctors made house calls then, and Dr. Kersh came and after examining me told Mom and Dad the bad news, lobar pneumonia, and that I needed to go into the hospital. I said no, that Mama was a better nurse than any of those working at the hospital. After begging and pleading with the doctor, he agreed to let me stay and would make visits out to the house twice a week. Mom and Dad didn't have insurance and did not have any money to pay for a hospital stay. That is why I was so persistent in not going. Mom and Dad already had two burdens on them, no money and my having pneumonia, and they did not need another one dragging them further down.

For the next four weeks, all I could do was lie in the bed, listen to the radio, and take medicine. I had missed half of the first semester of school and was looking forward to getting back for the second. I had just turned seventeen back in September and did not need to repeat the tenth grade. My plan was to go back in the second semester and work real hard to keep up and then make up for the work I missed in summer school.

The Sunday before Christmas Day, I felt I was almost over my sickness and that afternoon told Mom I wanted to go to church at the evening service. I was president of our youth group and I had been away from my duties long enough. Mom and Dad didn't think it was a good idea, but after an hour of convincing I won. I bundled up good and we went to church. By the time we arrived at the church, my fever was starting to come back on me. I didn't tell my parents for fear they would take me home. Shortly after church started, I was in the pulpit conducting youth business and about half way through, I collapsed! I was immediately taken home and put to bed. The doctor came to the house at ten o'clock that night and told us that I had a relapse of pneumonia.

The first week in January 1963, I finally was able to get out of bed with only light duty chores. By mid month we had moved back to Bryant and my plans for getting through the tenth grade this year were gone. I started talking to Mom and Dad about going into the Marines and complete my education that way and, besides, all my friends had either gone off to college or entered the service. Of course, it was a resounding *no*! I continued to try and convince them, but each time the answer was the same. During the middle of March, the discussion came up again and this time I said that if they didn't sign for me now, I would enlist on my own when I turned eighteen. Finally, they both agreed, and on March 28, 1963, I was sworn in the United States Marine Corps, and from that day forward, my life would change forever.

CHAPTER TWO

Boot Camp

The last Day at Home

It was 7:00 a.m. on Monday morning when I awakened, and Mom was in the kitchen just getting breakfast on the table. Dad had taken off work for the day and the three of us sat down to eggs, bacon, and some of mom's good ole catfish biscuits. If silence is golden, the three of us became very wealthy at the breakfast table that morning. The tension was very immense while we were eating and I could see Mom was doing all she could to hold back the tears. Dad broke the ice and said, "This is what you wanted. I hope you are happy." Mom couldn't hold back anymore and started crying. I was trying to console her when Dad said, "You have broken your mama's heart, look at her." Mom said, "No, he hasn't, I'm proud of him but I worry that he might go to war. That's why I hate to see him go." Consoling Mom, Dad said, "Maybe he won't, but if he does he will have the best training there is.; The Marines are the best." We all got ready and left to go over to my grandpa's where the whole gang was there to see me off.

All my aunts and uncles were there to wish me well. Everyone brought potluck for dinner and it was quite a wingding. I thought they were making way too much out of this event, but after all I was the first nephew to leave for the military. My aunts reminded me that I was a Patrick and I was to use my best manners while I was gone. My uncles were telling me what to expect at boot camp: like the drill instructors will get into your face and tell me I won't make it, stuff like that; and not to volunteer for anything. Everyone was serious about what they were saying to me, and I took it all in. After all, I had never been in the military before and most of them had. Time flies when you're having fun. It was finally time to go to the airport in Little Rock. After I said my goodbyes to my parents and they did likewise, I boarded the plane with an ache in my heart knowing I would not see them for a long time but was looking forward to getting to California. I had never been on an airplane and was anxious to experience the flight.

Marine Corps Recruit Depot (MCRD)

The flight out to San Diego was uneventful and a lot of fun. There were not very many passengers, so the flight attendants played cards with the three of us recruits. The trip from Little Rock took about six hours, including a layover in Dallas.

At San Diego, a very polite Marine Sergeant met us and asked who was in charge on the trip out and I told him, I was. He took the paperwork our recruiter gave me and told us to have a seat, that there were other flights coming in and we would all leave for the base together. He carried on a conversation with us like another one of the guys. We all thought boot camp was going to be a walk in the park. After about an hour, everyone was accounted for on the Sergeant's roster and we were told to get into the back of the truck. There were eighteen of us and all we could see was a pickup truck. That was the only transportation for the marines, so we all jumped in the back of that little pickup. We were packed in like sardines in a flat can. However, the trip was only about ten minutes, so it wasn't so bad. When the truck stopped, we all started to pile out of the truck, and this very polite sergeant turned into a, well to put it mildly, I thought a satanic spirit had entered into this man's body! He began shouting, "Did I tell you to disembark? Get back on the truck! That wasn't fast enough, out of the truck! Get back in the truck double time!" We must have got on and off that truck twenty times before he finally turned us over to the devil himself! By that time it was about nine-thirty in the evening. The *devil,* Sgt. Chandler, was the reception NCO (Non commissioned Officer) and did he receive! We were all in front of the reception center on the asphalt, and Sgt. Chandler was shouting, telling us to come to attention, shut up, and listen up. There were still some guys talking and he would run over to them, get right into their face, and say, "Did I not tell you to shut up, Private? From here on out, you do not open your mouth unless I tell you, do you understand, Private? When you do open your mouth, the first word out of your mouth is sir and the last word out of your mouth is sir. Do you understand, Privates?" We all said very weakly, "yes sir." Again, the sergeant started running to each one of us reminding us of what he had told us, "Sir, yes sir," we exclaimed. He said, "I can't hear you, girls" and we all repeated very loudly, "Sir, yes sir." Sgt. Chandler was still not satisfied; I still can't hear you, and again we repeated the phrase. This went on for over ten minutes. After the, sir, yes sir thing, we entered the receiving barracks, where we were issued linen for the bunks we were to sleep on. We then had to turn in all of our civilian attire (everything), even our watches and rings (only the ones married could keep their wedding bands). We were then issued one set of marine dungarees, one cover (cap), one Skivvies (underwear), one pair of boots, and toiletries. By this time, it was getting to be almost 11:00 p.m. Then we were told to hit the rack (go to bed). By this time, Sgt. Chandler had a reinforcement, which to this day I don't know who he was. When we were told to hit the rack, we were also told not to say a word; also, that everyone will get into the bed all at the same time. The first time we got into our racks it wasn't good enough, not everyone climbed in at the same time, so we had to get out of our bunks and do it again, and again, and again. I know we must have got out of those bunks, well, I lost count after ten times. Then the sergeant said, "Well, you all finally did it right; good night, privates"; "Sir, good night, sir," we answered, and the sergeant started shouting and saying things that would make a sailor blush, "Out of the racks *now*! I told you I did not want to hear a peep out of you! Out! Out! Out! We got out of the racks, and the sergeant told us to hit the rack and not a sound from anyone. This went on for about twenty minutes, because there was always one dumb ass that had to tell the sergeant good night. When the sergeant finally left us alone, it was after midnight and we were totally, mentally, and physically drained of energy. It did not take us long to fall asleep, but as I was drifting off I could not help but think of what I had left behind back home in Arkansas. I was an innocent boy who had joined an outfit where boys were not allowed. I would have to learn to be a man and leave the *boy* in these barracks. Remember that walk in the park thing; well, disregard! This was going to be the biggest challenge of my life, a long hard run up a very steep hill!

The first full day of boot camp came very early, 4:30 a.m. to be precise. We had ten minutes to shave, shower, and do other necessities. Then we stripped our racks down for the next group to arrive later in the day. There were two different sergeants today and these were our drill instructors (DIs): Sgt. James, a huge man in stature, about six feet five inches tall. He was lean and rock solid, not just a huge person but the largest *anything* I had ever seen. Then there was Sgt. Steed, just as lean and solid but about five feet eight inches in stature. A Mississippi Rebel who appeared not to like any one from anywhere, even Mississippi. He was a man that was well versed in martial arts and appeared to have the attitude, the bad don't mess with him, 'cause it would probably be their worst nightmare. We were told to get outside into formation and we would go eat breakfast. After the usual shouting and harassment, we marched to the chow hall, where we all had to play the "hurry up and wait" game for the morning meal. No one was allowed to sit down or touch their food until everyone had gone through the line and arrived at the long table designated. Once everyone was seated, and I might mention everyone had to sit at the same exact time (took several times), we had three minutes to eat at attention. Then it was off to the barber shop where everyone received the same tapered unique style of cut, high and tight! Then it was off to receive the rest of our clothing, toiletries, and all the other belongings the taxpayers had so freely given to the government so we would not have to go around naked defending them! By noon, we were so weary from carrying our gear around the base that we were all exhausted, and the day was only half over. I was wondering where I was going to get the energy, just to continue the day, and what the other 119 days would be like.

The rest of the week was like the first day, getting more tolerable every day: administrative stuff, retaking our physical exams, the dental clinic, Military Occupational Specialty test, (MOS), and shots and shots and more shots. I felt like a pin cushion that a seamstress uses when sewing, except that my cushions did not remain the same size. I could hardly sit down or raise my arms, and everyday I kept saying, "I hope there are no more shots."

On the last administrative day, the guys who did not graduate from high school were given the opportunity to take the GED, and I fell into this group. I was excited about this and welcomed the challenge because I regretted not completing high school and, besides, it was one of the promises I had made to my mother.

I passed my GED test with just above the minimum score and I was satisfied with that. Now I can think about going to college later when my enlistment was up. I scored very high on my MOS test and was happy about that, because I wanted to be a recon marine and they only take people who made above the ninety percentile range; luckily, I fell in that range. All I had to do now was qualify physically and mentally and that required being in the top one percent in the battalion. There were 580 men in a boot camp battalion. It meant only five people would be considered for recon. When I passed my GED exam, my attitude changed, and I was more confident that I would not only make it through the challenge of boot camp, but could also be in the top five percent and I also knew that it was time to bear down and get to work.

In the second week, drill instructors James and Steed were beginning to get tougher. Close order drill (COD) was the order of the days ahead. Running and Physical Training (PT) were incorporated as well. We were learning how to march, and if one person screwed up during COD, *everyone* paid the price. You see, COD was precision marching movements and tactics, and when one man made a mistake, it threw the entire platoon off time and out of sync. So, it was to the sandpits for PT, push-ups, sit-ups, pull-ups, duck walks, holding buckets of sand straight out and level, and if we didn't do these exercises up to the DI's standards we stayed there until we did, *all of us*! One night we stayed in the sandpits until 7:30 p.m. (1930 hours), and after that, we went for a two mile run. One more thing about the sandpits; there were these little critters called sand fleas. They would bite and make you itch and leave little whelps on you. You did not by any means slap at them, scratch yourself, or even act like you wanted to, otherwise we would be longer there digging a six-foot cubed hole to bury a sand flea. The DIs made the statement, "Sand fleas were doing a better job at what they do, than we were at doing what we were *supposed* to do, and deserved a decent burial for superior work above and beyond the call of duty." I suppose that statement was partly true at the time, because we were constantly doing something wrong to wind up there. I believe we buried five sand fleas in the second week alone and we made five trips to the sandpits. Two mile runs (sometimes more than two miles) morning, noon, and evening, PT scheduled at least twice a day (not counting the trips to the sandpits), and COD five to seven hours a day. My attitude was, at this rate, it would not take long to get in shape and reach my goal, and that was qualifying for recon.

The third week was almost a repeat of the second, except that there were less trips to the sandpits, a sign that we were doing better; and we could feel that we were also. The DIs were starting to bear down really hard and they were giving a few of us extra work and PT, literally picking on us. They made it obvious too, and told us they would do everything they could to wash us out. One of them was yours truly, and at first, I thought they were just picking on me. I started to take it personally and, as observed, there were three other recruits receiving the same treatment. I asked them what their MOS was going to be. All of them said recon and then we realized, they were probably ordered to give us this treatment to see if we could take it, not only physically but mentally as well. It was their job to break us if they could. At this time, the four of us decided to band together and help each other in all aspects and with encouragement. Forced Recon is the elite organization of the marines, right up there with the Navy SEALS who train together, to learn to be the best in the world. As a matter of fact, the two organizations worked together on some missions forming Special Operations groups. This is what I wanted. Nothing in the marines is guaranteed, even if you are qualified. You have to earn it step by step, you have to want it so much, you will do whatever it takes to get it. You have to know your strengths and utilize them to full capacity. Know your weaknesses so you can improvise in the proper manner, and use them to your advantage (in other words, when life deals you lemons, make lemonade);then adapt to the situation and overcome the objective and when you get it, you *know you have earned it*! This was going to be a battle of wills between the four of us and the two DIs. We were going to do our best to obtain our goal, and they were going to do their best to see how much we wanted it. We had the advantage. We had the DIs outnumbered by a hundred percent.

The fourth week, like the previous weeks, started on Sunday. In the Marine Corps boot camp, there was not very much free time. After morning chow, we would march to church where all Protestant denominations were in the same building at the same time and dismissed at 0900 hours. We then marched back to our platoon area, and donned the PT uniform, went for a minimum three mile run, then PT for an hour. Then we marched to chow and back to barracks for free time, from 1200 to 1700 hours. It was during this time that we used to get caught up on our letter reading and writing, and getting uniforms ready for the week (we washed our own clothes), shined our own boots, and then took care of personal things. From 1700 to 1930 hours, there was *field* day of the barracks and heads (bathrooms) and then inspection. Of course, most of the time, we failed inspection and had to do it all over again. I believe most of the time, there wasn't anything wrong, as much as the DIs wanted to keep us busy until taps (lights out). As you can see, there were not any days off; even Saturday was a full scheduled workday.

On Monday morning of the fourth week, at 0600 hours, after a four mile run, we were on the snapping in range, preparing for rifle qualification. This was an area where we practiced sighting in at a target, without ammunition. We practiced getting into the sitting, offhand (standing), kneeling, and prone positions. We stayed in these positions for what sometime seemed like an eternity. I have always been a good marksman, but this dry firing was more boring than watching paint dry. By Wednesday, going through this from 0630 to 1300 hours, we were ready for this week to be over, and get to live firing. We learned nomenclature, by breaking down the weapon, and putting it back together again. We must have done this about ten times a day. I got so good at it, I believe I could have broke my rifle down and put it back together blindfolded. I wasn't told to and neither was anyone else, contrary to what you may have heard or seen in the movies.

This week was also set aside for familiarization with all other weaponry the marines used: the .45 caliber pistol, the Browning automatic rifle (BAR), the M-60 machine gun, the .50 caliber machine gun, and the M-26 fragmentation hand grenade. We would see a demonstration, then had the opportunity to fire the weapon, and toss grenades (two). All of this happened on the last day of the week, Saturday.

On Monday morning of the fifth week, we were finally on the live firing range. Like the previous week, the morning and noon meals were brought to us. We practiced from the two hundred, three hundred, and five hundred yard lines (the same way we would qualify). We went through this once in the morning, and afternoon, and a live firing range is not a good place to be in the summer months. The morning session was not so bad; however, the afternoon sun in California can be brutal at times, especially with the humidity. The temperature at MCRD in the summer at most training sites can reach the high nineties; adding the heat index factor, along with the full combat gear we were wearing each day, would make the heat well over 100 degrees. A person had to stay well hydrated or he would go down, especially when there was no shade, so drinking a lot of water was the order of the day. If you could hold it, one quart of water was ordered, per hour. The Marines did not cancel training due to extreme heat or cold. Their philosophy was: *suck it up*, do what you have to do to adapt and overcome because that is exactly what has to be done in combat situations.

As I stated earlier, I had always been a good marksman and getting the hang of shooting on a firing range seemed natural to me. Though this environment was a new experience, I was hitting the bull's-eye all week, most of the time. When I had my weapon zeroed correctly for all of the distances, it was easy. When you hit the target, the guys working in the butts (pulling and marking targets) would mark the target with a three-inch round disc. If you hit in the black bull's-eye, the disc was white, and the disc was black on any other part of the target. When I hit the center of the bull, it was a good challenge for me to try and shoot the disc off the target, which I did on numerous occasions. That's all there was to it. Qualification day (Friday) was no different than the other days of shooting, but this time it was for the record. A perfect score was 250. Each shooter had fifty rounds; maximum scoring was: in the bull= five points, close in but out of the bull's-eye=four, then three, and last, two.

I only had eight rounds out of the bull on qualification Day; the rest were in the bull's-eye. I fired 242, which is expert. In our platoon, out of sixty people, there were twenty-three that fired expert, and no one failed to qualify. We were the only platoon in the battalion to qualify in every one. We were really proud of ourselves, and the DIs were thinking our platoon had a legitimate shot at being the Regimental honor platoon (best in the regiment). I might make mention of the fact that I was not the highest shooter that day. There were two ahead of me, Pvt. Tolliver, from Mississippi, who shot a perfect 250, and Pvt. Sylvan from Colorado, who fired a 243. Both of the men were recon bound as well as myself and Pvt. Reed from San Diego, who shot 239, on qualification day. The DIs were upset that there were nine people who qualified but with a low score, so after the firing range that afternoon, it was back to the sandpits for another round. The DIs were never satisfied with our performance, regardless of how well we did. There was always room for improvement. *They demanded perfection!*

Saturday brought a welcome change; for the first time in five weeks, we could have visitors for four hours, from 1000 to 1400 hours. My parents had moved to California, so I had visitors. It was the first time in five weeks we had any communication from the outside, except for letters. My first thought was to refuse visiting with my parents because I did not want to lose focus of my goal, but my emotions were much stronger that day.

It was great to see Mom and Dad, and they were glad to see me. I could not go off the base but could go anywhere on it (except for restricted areas of course). So we took a short tour and to my surprise it was pretty pleasant, since all I had seen of MCRD was the parade field, sandpits, and some of the field training areas; so I, along with them, was seeing it for the first time. They were surprised to see that I had gained my weight back from the pneumonia I had prior to enlistment. When I enlisted, my weight was down to 145, and now it was up to 172. I was in the best shape of my life and I felt really great about myself. Mom fed me fried chicken and mashed potatoes she had brought from home. Man, was it good! I stuffed myself to misery! After we talked and visited, it was time to leave and go back to work, but it was a welcome sight to see my parents, because it would be another seven weeks before I would see them again. You see, back in the sixties, there were only two visitations in marine boot camp: at the end of the fifth week, and on graduation day.

Weeks six and seven found us in the field for the land navigation classes and practical application. After classes, we practiced plotting azimuths on the map, shooting back azimuths, etc. We were given grid coordinates which we had to plot on the map, shoot the azimuth with a compass, and march to that place successfully within a certain time. The destinations would be marked with a letter or number, and only the instructors knew what they were. When we reported back, we told them the number, and they would tell us if we were right or wrong. This was a lot of fun, because it was the first time in any event so far that the DIs were not breathing down our necks and in our face. We were on our own. We had day and night missions and some were more than three miles in distance.

There were five day and five night missions and you received ten points for each successful mission. The passing score for this course was seventy out of a possible hundred, so you had to have seven successful missions. The platoon did great on this course, qualifying everyone with an overall average score of ninety. Each individual had their own missions. You did not have a team on these missions (though we did practice in teams at first). Everyone in the platoon had to pass this course on their own.

The eighth and ninth weeks were hand-to-hand combat, bayonet, fighting with pugil sticks, and indoctrination classes. The tenth week was individual PT tests. President Kennedy was our commander and chief at that time, and he was there to observe. The President stood within six feet of me, and I was very nervous about doing something stupid. Anytime the President of the United States was present at any event, it was a big deal. Well, all I can say is, you better not mess up or there would be hell to pay later. The PT test consisted of sit-ups, push-ups, pull-ups, three hundred yard dash individually, and running three miles in platoon formation. All events were to be performed in full combat gear. It was grueling; no rest in between all individual events, and the heat with all that gear was terrible. The amount of repetitions in the calisthenics was not as important as completing the time of each event (two and one half minutes). After the calisthenics was the three hundred yard dash, a fast walk to the track, and waiting for the starter to say go. We had sixty seconds to complete the run. After all the exercises, three hundred yards was hard to accomplish in one minute. If a person failed to complete any of the four part individual PT test, they had to retake the entire test later that afternoon; if they did not pass on the second chance, they had to recycle back to the seventh week with another platoon. This was the case with any training or event. Back then, you could not graduate from boot camp without getting a go (pass) on every part of your training. After the individual events, the PT test was not over by a long shot. There was the three mile run in platoon formation. Each platoon had thirty-two minutes for the last man to cross the finish line. If any person crossed the line later than the time allotted, the entire platoon got a no-go, (failed); and this part of the test was not retaken. This event was to see how well the DIs prepared their recruits. All of our training was important, but this, along with the COD competition later that week, was probably the most important. These two events (under extreme mental and physical stress and pressure) tested our endurance, stamina, focus, attention to detail, demeanor, discipline, and the Semper Fidelis (Always Faithful) spirit to ourselves, our comrades, the Marine Corps, and the United States of America.

The Close Order Drill competition (precision marching) was more mentally stressful than any of the other events. If everyone did not stay focused throughout the entire event, it would be easy to make a mistake, so being focused and staying disciplined was the order of the day. There were thirty-six platoons in the regimental competition and it was our goal to be the best. When the competition was over (our final completion of our training), my platoon had a perfect score (no faults), the only platoon to accomplish the task in twelve years. Thank *God*, there would be no more sandpits!

The eleventh week of boot camp went back to administrative stuff, and practicing for graduation exercises and awards ceremonies. We would also find out our MOS, and where we would be going after our infantry training. Every person that enlists in the Marines is primarily a rifleman, regardless of his MOS. We were not called marines in boot camp, because we had not earned the title; however, we were called a lot of other names I won't mention, and if we were lucky, we would be called what we were: *Privates.*

I remember when Drill Instructor Steed summoned me to the duty hut, something that did not happen unless you were in trouble. Privates Tolliver, Sylvan, and Reed were called as well, and we figured it was going to be another harassment session. When we all reported to Sgt. Steed in the proper manner, "Sir, Private Reeves reporting to the Drill Instructor as ordered, sir." Sgt. Steed hesitated, then with a loud voice said, "Well, you scumbags made it, you are going to recon school. *God* help all of you, 'cause you are going to need Him! At ease." Then we saw the other side of Drill Instructor Steed when he very softly said, "I am proud of the entire platoon, and I am especially proud of the four of you. In every cycle of boot camp, there are one or two individuals the men look up to: Men who set the standards high and always leading and encouraging the least to bring out their best to make them set their goals high. You are those four men, dismissed!" When we left the duty hut, we were jumping for joy at what our DI had said to us, but especially for the way he said it. My thoughts were confirmed: Marine Corps Drill Instructors *are* human!

Regimental honor is something that all marine recruits long for, but as time continues in boot camp, most think it is out of reach for them, and just getting through training would be a great accomplishment for them; and it is. However, some have the attitude that mediocrity is not acceptable. Such was Private Oscar Romie Reed. He was the high school all-American football player from San Diego. He was recruited by some of the biggest colleges in our great nation, UCLA, USC, Texas, Notre Dame, Alabama, to mention a few, but choose to serve his country instead. That says a lot for a man who knows what his real priorities are. He made the statement several times, "If you want to succeed in life, help as many people get what they want in life, and participate in something greater than yourself putting forth 110 percent and you will be a success, knowing you have done your best and helped someone along the way." How true that statement is: I know it inspired me and a lot of other people. Oscar was awarded the highest honor a boot recruit can receive: Regimental Honor Marine. Private Tolliver and I were runners' up for regimental honor marine and received promotions to Private First Class, E-2. Our platoon, Platoon number 322, won the regimental honor platoon (there were thirty-six platoons in the regiment) winning fifteen of the sixteen competition events. The standards were set very high for the regimental honor platoon. For instance, even if a platoon won all the events but more than two men were not able to finish training with the platoon they started with, for any reason (except death of a parent), that platoon was eliminated from the regimental honor qualification.

Graduation went off without a hitch. Dozens of dignitaries were there with well over a thousand spectators looking on to see their loved one graduate. Two of them were my parents and it was really great to see them again. I felt so proud. After graduation, we had six hours' liberty and could go off post, so Mom and Dad took me on a short tour of San Diego, and to the place where they lived. It was there that I had my second home-cooked meal in twelve weeks, and again I stuffed myself! By then it was time to go back to base and the platoon area, where we would load our gear onto buses bound for Camp Pendleton, fifty miles away. As the coach left, most of the guys were shouting obscenities to the drill instructors and talking bad about them, at how much they hated all of them. While the majority of them were just letting off steam, I sat quietly, thinking of how wrong they were. The training, guidance, and leadership these special men provided us with made me grateful to be a part of the finest organization in the world. Semper Fi!

Camp Pendleton

Camp Pendleton is the largest Marine Corps base in the world and the second largest military installation in the world; only the Army's Fort Hood is larger, only ninety square miles.

Upon arrival at Camp Pendleton, two drill sergeants entered the bus and said, "Okay, Marines, off the bus, step lively!" I felt so proud; it was the first time in our enlistment that we were addressed as Marines. It meant, by completing boot camp training, we had earned the title. Hell, we all felt proud, but this did not mean training would be lax. This was infantry training, and they had four weeks to turn us into a sound fighting unit. Regardless of your MOS, be it a clerk, supply, infantryman, recon, or in the band, every marine had to go through the Infantry Training Regiment (ITR).

In boot camp, we trained from a platoon level. Here at ITR, we would learn at the four man level (fire team), twelve man squad platoon level, and the company level. We learned how to advance on the enemy at the company level, but using the fire team tactic approach, and from different directions, called diversions. Most of us from the old boot camp platoon were split up into different platoons and companies. There was good reasoning behind this; in combat, if you transferred to another unit, you would not know anyone. The marine philosophy was, get used to it early in your career.

The part of Camp Pendleton was a place called Camp San Onifree located more on the south side of Pendleton. "Old Smoky" (not the song) is located here at San Onifree, a 1,955 foot mountain, that we would grow accustomed to as much as the sandpits of San Diego.

Monday morning brought reveille at 0430 hours, and a quick shave and dress for inspection brought us to formation at 0450 hours. After inspection, Sgt. Clark (one of the drill sergeants) decided it was time to get acquainted with "Ole Smokey," since we were new to the area and knew that we were eager to get a closer look at it; s-u-r-r-e, we were . . . After a two mile run to the foot of the mountain, we started up the mountain (still in double time), and Sgt. Clark said, "Any Marine who makes it to the top without stopping will get a week off." Well, you should have seen all of us breaking out of formation in an attempt to make it to the summit. PFC Sleeper (a Native American) and I were leading the pack. After we had been running for about five minutes, we looked back and there was no one around us; we thought we were the only ones who wanted a week off, so we kept on going. When we got about halfway to the top, we met the other drill sergeant, Sgt. Finger, who made us turn around and go back down the hill. There was no way they were going to let us get to the summit, at least not today, and everyone heard the rest of what Sgt. Clark had said, "That is if you can get past Sgt. Finger." Sleeper and I didn't hear that because we were in a hurry to get that week off; it was a reminder for us to listen completely to what was being said before going off half-cocked! The rest of the day and for the next two days were filled with classes, PT, and demonstrations on how things should be done and how they should not be done. The company would then put all this together by performing these tactics. The basic combat infantry tactics were: fire team, squad team, platoon level, and company assaults (frontal, echelon right and left, diversionary tactics, and the suicidal assault) and also the live fire infiltration course, land navigation, night vision tactics. The final week of the ITR was spent in an area of Camp Pendleton called Case Springs (which were in the foothills of the San Bernardino mountain range), putting all of these tactics together in situational combat simulation. After the war games, we marched back to San Onifree, which was twenty-eight miles from where we were. That march marked the end of our training at ITR and, yes, most of the company did make it to the top of "Ole Smokey" some of us more than once. After sixteen weeks of some of the hardest training in the world, on some of the roughest terrain in the states, the initial training was over and some of us had twenty days' leave. Those of us who qualified for force recon school had to report to Camp Delmar to undergo a two-week course of recon/SEAL qualification before our leave started. If you did not wash out of this two-week course, you were qualified to attend force recon training school and/or SEAL training school. *I thought boot camp was hard!*

I did not have to report to Del Mar until the following Monday morning, so I decided to call Dad to pick me up so that I could relax at their house until Sunday night. PFC Amick Sleeper (I called him "Chief") asked if he could tag along with me, and of course I said yes. Chief is an Arapaho Indian from Oklahoma. We were good buddies all through ITR; he also had to report to Camp Del Mar, Monday morning. On Saturday, we went to a movie downtown called Cleopatra, starring Elizabeth Taylor and Richard Burton; quite a movie for folks who like that sort of thing. Then we caught the bus over to the San Diego zoo, which we heard was the largest in the world and I believe it. I went back there on five or six occasions and still haven't seen it all. On Sunday morning, we woke up and decided to go to church because we had attended only the chapel at the base for the last sixteen weeks; it would be good to get out and meet new people for a change. After church, the four of us went to eat in a real restaurant; the first in a long time. On Sunday night, Chief and I decided to leave for Camp Del Mar; we didn't want to take the chance of being late by leaving on Monday morning, so we reported in early.

The Sounding of the Bell

Monday morning was finally here and reveille was at 0430 hours; the time had become routine for the chief and me: formation at

0500 hours in the PT uniform for what the training NCOs called the morning stroll. Camp Del Mar, part of Camp Pendleton, was across interstate five freeway (the ocean side of the camp), with five miles of oceanfront beach. It was explained to us that the beaches were where ninety percent of our training would be conducted. There were four training NCOs: Gunnery Sergeant Phillips (Gunny), who was senior training NCO, Navy Chief Petty Officer Joiner (Chief), Staff Sergeant Mann, and Sergeant Daniels. It was their job to run us into the ground, into the sand, in the water, under the water, in the air, nonstop for the next eight days and most of the time at nights until we couldn't take it anymore and rang the bell. I need to explain the ringing of the bell. The bell was located outside company headquarters on a pedestal. When a Marine or Sailor felt like he could not continue the training due to physical, mental, or psychological limitations, he could ring the bell and leave the training immediately, getting an unsatisfactory for the course, disqualifying him from recon for two years (this is what we call washing out). If you rang the bell, that was it! No more chances, no exceptions!

We started running in formation at 0500 hours and we were still running at 0630 hours when Chief Joiner told us that we only had another five miles to go until chow. There were 122 of us running and everyone of us fell out of formation that morning. At about 0635 hours, Chief Joiner re-formed us into formation and told us, if anyone else fell out of the run, we would get an unsatisfactory, and you were only allowed two un-sats for the two weeks of the training. At the end of the run, twenty-three men rang the bell. They had to leave the area immediately. In only two hours of training we were down to ninety-nine; how many more would ring the bell, I didn't know. I only knew, neither Amick nor I were going to be the ones, even if I had to carry him, or he had to carry me. This was *Hell* Week, and the training NCOs were running right along with us and if they could do it, we could do it. Together all the way! Semper Fi!

After morning chow, immediately we ran to the beach where we started running one hundred meter wind sprints back and forth for over an hour and a half. Running in the sand is extremely hard; the boots we had on would sink down to the ankles and, first thing, the calves of your legs would burn, then the thighs get weak, then your chest hurts, your belly, every part of your body aches; you feel like you can't put one step in front of the other, and you want to stop! Then it hits you; all that great breakfast you had comes up. Oh, what a horrible feeling! But you don't dare quit; you keep going until the Training NCO says stop! Problem is, you don't know when that is going to be. After the upchucking, it's just a matter of time before you start to lose control of some of your body functions; I think you get the picture, but you don't dare stop!

Then it was in the water after the wind sprints. Man, what a relief after all that running. It gave us a chance to cool off; just to relax in that cool salt water was such a relief. After about five minutes of that we were ordered to swim to a buoy about a hundred yards out. There we had to form a wide circle around the buoy and tread water until further notice. I knew we were going to be out there for a while, because there was a boat not too far away. Chief Joiner told us, if we see our buddy in trouble, we were to take him to the boat. What seemed like an hour, but was only around fifteen to twenty minutes, the first man went down, and one by one over the course of an hour, until we couldn't take any more. After that we were called everything but a human being; Chief Joiner was the only person in the water, while he was calling us maggots, sissyies, pussies (and those were the nice words), saying none of us will make it through; then he told us to get out of the boat and swim to the shore. We ran back to the company area where we cleaned ourselves up and got ready for the noon meal. When we arrived at the mess hall, we were so tired we could hardly raise our forks to eat. We were told not to eat fast, and we only had ten minutes to complete our meal. After noon chow we ran back to the company area. Then we were told that training did not start until tomorrow; this is a short day, so use the rest of the day to mentally prepare for the next seven days because it will be nonstop. Our physical and mental endurance will be tested twenty-four hours of the day; also to get our letter writing and phone calls done because there will not be time after the day is over, because training starts at 0100 hours in the morning. Well, that went over well, as you can imagine, but we all asked for this and we would get a lot more than we bargained for. After the noon meal there were another thirty-five who rang the bell. Now we were down to sixty-four, almost half, and the thought ran through my mind, "how many more would we lose before it was over and would I be one of them." I looked over at the chief (Amick) and said, "You got to help me, man!" He said, "We got to help each other!"

The day started on time, 0100 hours as promised, with all the training NCOs on deck and the mental harassment started. It was time to maintain control and go with the flow; it was all business maintaining the attitude, just another day at the office. The exercises, the running, the duck walks, the bear claws, wind sprints all in the sand; the water exercises, the swimming, the snorkeling, and the mental harassment during and in between for fourteen hours straight everyday was bearing down hard. Something happened the third day; the training was getting more intense and longer, but it got easier. Some of us were getting conditioned to the treatment that we were receiving. On Saturday at 0100 hours began the nonstop forty-eight-hour hell day. After it was over, only twenty-eight of us remained. *Hell week* was over. The chief and I had made it through. The next four days would be filled up with classes, of the classified nature, outprocessing, and reporting to our permanent duty stations; and then twenty days leave. What a relief!

CHAPTER THREE

Permanent Duty Assignment

The chief and I were assigned to the same unit, and it was only a half mile from where we were, still on Camp Del Mar; First Marine Division, Force Recon Marine Special Operations Battalion (nicknamed "The Walking Dead"). When we reported to headquarters, we found out our company and platoon, Bravo Company, first platoon. We were handed our orders for paratrooper school and leave papers. We were to report to the U S Army Paratrooper Training School, Ft. Benning, GA, on the August 15. This worked out great; we had twenty days' leave and then we would have four days to report to school. The reason for the rush in attending jump school: in order to be qualified for this unit, you have to be jump qualified and scuba qualified. Without these two qualifications, you are a washout and would be transferred to a rifle company. After what we had gone through, I didn't believe anything the Army or the Navy threw at us was going to phase us. Boy, were we wrong! I just threw that in to give respect to the Army; however, jumping out of a plane at twelve hundred feet was frightening at first, to say the least.

I made a stopover in Arkansas to see everyone and get them up to date on what was going on with me and to find out what was going on with them. All of my friends had gone to college or in the service as well, except for Charlie; he too was in the service, the Army National Guard. We rode around in his car catching up on old times. I stayed at my grandpa's house in Benton, where all my relatives came and visited. It was really good to see everyone and to be back home again. Duty calls though and eventually it was time to leave. Instead of continuing my trip to Ft. Benning by plane, Charlie wanted to drive me, so I said yes. This would give me a little more time with my friend.

There were all branches of the military in our training company, mostly Army Rangers and Special Forces personnel. Seventeen of us were Marines. We hit the ground running at Ft. Benning, from daylight to dark. Running was the order of the day, and for the next three and a half days they ran us into the ground. This was jump school and for over a week we had not seen anything that resembled a parachute. Then the obstacle courses were incorporated with the running, from daylight till dark with only short breaks every couple of hours. The classroom training started on what we had to know and how it would be performed at the school. Slides of life, repelling off cliffs, out of helicopters, as well as climbing up a ninety degree bluff, how to pack a parachute, and of course jumping out of perfectly good airplanes! As we would complete these tasks in the classrooms, and were tested on paper, it was time to put what we learned to the test by practical application. After eight weeks of this and our jumps (one day jump and one night jump), we had completed the school and became jump qualified and received our jump wings. After all the building up of the jumps and making a big deal of the whole thing, it wasn't so bad. As a matter of fact, it turned out to be (that first jump) one of the greatest thrills I would ever have.

Back in California, Mom and Dad had moved to San Clemente. Both got civil service jobs, Mom in the laundry at Camp Pendleton, Dad at the Marine Air Wing at El Toro in Santa Ana at the base service station. When time allowed, I would go to their house, but it was short-lived, because the word came down to move out!

Back at Camp Del Mar, my unit was getting ready for mobilization in four weeks to Okinawa, where we would become part of the Third Marine Division; however, the seventeen of us that had returned from jump school were left behind to complete Scuba School. After the five weeks of scuba, we were put on a commercial flight to Honolulu, HI, where the ship my unit was on docked to take on supplies for the trip to the Far East. This was going to be another new experience; I had never been on a ship or out in the middle of the ocean before. I was hoping I didn't get seasick!

The USS Breckenridge was a huge troop carrier that could quarter 2,500 troops. I didn't know how many marines were aboard, except that there were a lot of us. The trip to Okinawa would take fifteen days from Hawaii, and about the third day, I started to get sick to my stomach; I wasn't upchucking, just real nauseated. I never did throw up, but most of the guys did. About the eleventh or twelfth day, we arrived at the port of Yokohama, Japan. I wasn't sick anymore. They called it, "Getting my sea legs." Something else was going on, though. I guess everyone who was living back on November 22, 1963, remembers where they were and what they were doing on that fatal day in Dallas, Texas. When we first heard about the assassination of President Kennedy, it was November 23 (which would be the same day, twenty-four hours ahead by Japan time). We were tied up at the port of Yokohama. That was a sad, sad day for all of us. Thinking back on the event, I remember back in boot camp, only a few months prior, that the President stood only a few feet from me during my PT test, and now he was dead; what was our country coming to? We left Yokohama and arrived three days later in Naha, Okinawa.

Okinawa

The buses were waiting on us when we arrived at Naha. We were going to the northern part of the island called Camp Schwab. We were isolated from the rest of the division due to the classified training missions we were to perform. We were settled in about four days when training was supposed to start in full swing, but due to the assassination of the president, the flag at half-mast, training was limited; so for the next three weeks, we had a lot of inspections, COD, and PT. A lot of PT!

On Christmas Day of 1963, it was the first Christmas of many I was away from home. In the past, I was too busy to think of home, but with nothing to do, I was really homesick. There weren't any cell phones or computers back then, so you just had to make the best of it. S.Sgt. Dan White, my team leader, came over to cheer me up. He said he wanted to go to town and wanted someone to go with him. The chief and I went into town with him, and watching the local culture and the people of Okinawa was quite fascinating. Here I was in a strange country and it dawned on me, "If I am going to have to live among these nice folks, I need to communicate with them." While a lot of the locals spoke some English, a lot more did not and I wanted to know what they were all about; however, the men and women who fought the Japanese in World War II would probably have an entirely different attitude than this. As we walked on, observing, there was this place called a Dojo. I asked S.Sgt. White (since he was on his second tour) what the meaning of the word was; he told me, it was a place where people studied the martial arts. That was for me. I thought, if we ever had to go into combat, it just might come in handy. I commenced to walk through the door as S.Sgt. White said, "No-o-o-o!"

As soon as I crossed the threshold, I got knocked on my ass! I was dragged out of the dojo and this Okinawan said to me, "You, no come in!" Then he left and went back into the dojo.

S.Sgt. White said, "I tried to tell you not to go in there. You cannot go into a dojo in Okinawa when class is in session, and when you can, you must take your shoes off and bow when entering and again to the master."

I asked him, "How do you know this?"

S.Sgt. White said, "Because, Corporal, I learned the same way you did!" The chief was down the street buying souvenirs, and we decided to catch up with him and call it a day. On the island of Okinawa (also called "The Rock" among the American military), there was only Cinderella Liberty (until midnight) and even though it was early, I had seen enough of "The Rock" for one afternoon. I knew where I wanted to go on my next liberty and it was at that dojo.

Back at Camp Schwab, we decided to go to the NCO Club (noncommissioned officer) and see if any of the guys were there. While there, S.Sgt. White bought "The Chief" and me a beer. It would be my first taste of alcohol and I was nervous about it. S.Sgt. White picked up on it and asked, "You've never drank alcohol before, have you, Corporal?"

"No," I said.

He said to me, "Well, just take it easy and limit yourself to just one, two at the most and you will be okay." The beer tasted good, something different, almost mesmerizing; I could see why some people could get hooked on it. We had our two drinks and returned to the barracks. On the next day, "The Chief" and I decided to rent a cab and see some of the sites of "The Rock." Most of the island was beautiful, and it was hard to believe that eighteen years earlier one of the bloodiest battles in history had taken place there. The people of Okinawa were very nice to us and appeared glad that we were there. When we arrived back at camp, "The Chief" and I went to Special Services and enrolled in language courses, Japanese and Vietnamese. Vietnam was starting to heat up more, and even though no one had said anything official, the scuttlebutt was going around, not a matter of if but when we would be over there in the middle of it, so learning some of the language was, I thought, very appropriate; I also felt if I were going to be in a country where the official language was not English, then I needed to know what these people were saying about me. On the next day, "The Chief" and I went back to Gotimba (the town where the dojo was) and after entering the dojo properly, we asked if we could take some classes. We explained to Master Sakimoto that due to our training regimen we would not be able to follow a training cycle but would make as many sessions as possible. He said he was used to working with American servicemen and understood and welcomed us to the dojo. He set us up to attend classes on Monday, Wednesday, and Friday, from 1800 to 2000 hours. He also made it firm, not to be late. We could also attend Saturday afternoons as well to make up for the days that we had to miss due to our training. Language classes were from 1900 to 2100 hours on Tuesday and Thursday, and on Saturday from 1000 to 1200 hours; you can see that what free time I had was pretty well filled up. I would be able to make this schedule just fine for about a month. In January 1964, we were scheduled to move out to Mount Fuji, Japan, for cold weather survival training for four weeks, then to the island of Luzon (in the Philippines) for escape and evasion training for thirty days. After that, we would return to "The Rock." By the end of March, we would be back at Camp Schwab until August. We would then be scheduled to be with the Navy from August to December, afloat in the Pacific as the Southeast Asia's region 911 force. During this time, if anything happened that threatened any of our allies in the region, we were the first responders.

On the first Monday after Christmas, my team started Sniper school. The course was initially four weeks and there was follow-up training every six months. This was a combination of classroom and practical application. The weapon we used back then was the Remington, 30.06 bolt actions, a forty-six-inch barrel rifle (*not* your ordinary deer rifle). We used an eight-power scope. The starlight magnification scope was used for night missions. When properly zeroed, the rifle is accurate up to two thousand meters. At that time, there were more powerful weapons in our arsenal but none more durable or accurate. Because of the type of terrain we were going up against, the 30.06 was lighter and more maneuverable for the conditions. The Marine sniper creed "One Shot, One Kill" is what he lived by. His life and the life of the person with him depended on that one shot!

The Team

I can't go on without talking about my team, the greatest guys there ever lived.

S.Sgt. Dan White, Team Leader (AKA: Skipper), from Buffalo, NY, and a good friend; career marine, led by example, always helpful but firm. If you were right he went to bat for you; if you were wrong, look out! Big on training, Sgt. Striker was that type of leader. We all looked up to him. He had been in the Corps for twelve years and was a Korean war veteran. He spoke Japanese, Korean, and Vietnamese fluently. Specialty: Demolitions/intelligence.

Sgt. Don Reeves, Asst. Team Leader (AKA: The Wolf / Skip), from Bryant, AR; believed in training, the more the better. He always put the team first, making sure they had what they needed. Believed in getting inside their heads, making sure they were okay and on the ready. Wanted to make the military a career and attain the rank of Sergeant/Major Spoke broken Japanese and Vietnamese. Specialty: Sniper/Weapons/intelligence.

Cpl. Amick Sleeper (AKA: The Chief /Little Beaver), a Native American from Gary, OK. He always had a good thing to say about everyone he met. He was my closest friend. He did *not* like to be called a redskin; he would get killing mad. His dream was to travel the U.S. extensively when out of the service. Spoke fluent Spanish and French and broken Vietnamese. Specialty: Sniper/Tracker/Weapons/intelligence.

L/Cpl. Tommy Nettleton, from Clearwater, Florida. He came from the Second Marine Division at Camp LeJeune, NC. He was the older brother to former New York Yankees third baseman, Greg Nettleton. His dream was to see his brother play in the Yankee Stadium. Spoke fluent Spanish and broken Vietnamese. Specialty: Demolitions/intelligence.

L/Cpl. Chitchester B. Hays (AKA: The Scrounge/Lover Boy), from Harlan County, KY. Claimed to be a direct descendant of former President Hays; could drink anyone under the table and recite the alphabet backwards without a stammer. His goal in life was to make love to one thousand women before the age of thirty; at the age of nineteen, he claimed to have one-hundred twenty under his belt.

He had more guts than any man I have ever known. Spoke French and Japanese. Specialty: Weapons/intelligence.

PFC Jimmy Hatfield (AKA: Money Bags/Stockbroker), from Jackson, TN; the smallest man in the team at just five feet seven. Claimed to be related to the Hatfields who feuded with the McCoys for so long and had the stories to go with it. His goal in life was to be a stockbroker on Wall Street. Spoke French and Vietnamese. Specialty: Communications/intelligence.

Petty Officer, Second Class, Bobby Hopper (AKA: Hoppy), from Redmond, CA; the only college graduate in the team. Hoppy was the man we looked out for at all times. We looked up to him because he went through two boot camps, once in the Navy, and in order to become a Marine Corpsman, he had to go through Marine boot camp too. His goal was to attend medical school at UCLA and become a Medical Doctor. Spoke fluent French, Russian, Chinese, Japanese, Portuguese, and Vietnamese. Specialty: Medical Corpsman.

The seven of us became a band of brothers. When one was happy, we were all happy for him, and when one hurt, we hurt right along with him. We looked out for, and protected each other, and when one got into a barroom fight, we were there to keep it fair. We shared our food, our dreams, and our goals in life; joked together, laughed together, cried together, and partied together! We knew each other's job almost as well as they did, and we made a pact, if we got separated from each other, we would never forget each other. Only three of us would complete our tour overseas: The Chief, Lover Boy, and me. There will be more on that later.

Mount Fuji, Japan

We left Okinawa, January 29, 1964, for Japan aboard the USS *Cavalier*. It normally takes only three days' steaming time, but the Navy's training site is at sea, so it would be a five-day trip. When we arrived in Yokohama, we boarded a bus for the two hour trip to the base at Mt. Fuji. I was surprised that they drove on the left side of the road; I thought only the British drove on the *wrong* side. As I stared out the window of the bus looking at the countryside, the scenic beauty was breathtaking. Japan is a beautiful country. I could not wait to get liberty and visit some of the sites. Before we left the ship, we could see the mountain in the distance. It was glorious, so majestic. As we first approached the mountain by sea from the south side, about one third of it was snow covered; and as we gradually changed directions to enter the harbor from the west, more of the mountain became covered with snow. The north side of Mt. Fuji is completely snow covered, which is exactly where our base camp was. Before I continue, I must tell you some facts about Mt. Fuji, so please bear with me.

Mt. Fuji is a volcano; as a matter of fact, geologists say it is the most perfect volcano in the world. It is inactive and has not erupted in over three hundred years. It is Japan's highest peak at 12,388 ft. The average temperature in the summer time (August), on the summit, is forty-one degrees Fahrenheit with strong constant winds blowing thirty to forty miles per hour. Winters on the summit can drop to an average low of −15 degrees Fahrenheit and a wind chill down to −35 degrees. At the base of the north side of the mountain, we had temperatures of zero to ten degrees with wind chills to minus ten degrees. The mountain was discovered by Buddhist monks on a journey in AD 663. The mountain was used by Samurai Warriors as a training camp in ancient times, and now by the US Marines.

Our base camp was a tent city, including chow halls, laundry, Post Exchange (PX), NCO Club, Recreation hall, and the billeting areas. Snow and muddy streets everywhere, but that was to be expected.

During the first three days at base camp, the plan of action for training was lined out for the seventeen days of winter survival training. My team, along with ten other teams, was to seek out and destroy as many of the opposing forces as possible, while traveling to destinations of twenty clicks and return to our original jumping off point. Each team had a different jump point and different destination. If we were captured by the opposing force, we were to escape and evade them. In other words, each individual in this situation was on his own for the rest of the mission, or he might get lucky and find the rest of his team. We had a plan "B" that we discussed among ourselves. Never leave a member of the team behind; if one or more of us got captured, the rest of the team would disorganize and create as much chaos by any means necessary, while one member of the team would free us. It worked! The team decided to put the plan to work before we left on the mission. We drew straws to see who would be the captive; and it was "Money Bags." It took us only forty minutes to free him and take evasive action while inflicting a crippling blow to the opposing force. I might add that the opposing force was a rifle company of 250 troops and that we were able to disable half of their forces; and the disabling factor helped us to complete the rest of our mission successfully. We were the only recon team that successfully completed the mission, which was all of us together reaching back to the starting point. We adapted, we improvised, and we overcame the situation.

We got pretty hungry, though; each of us had only five days' rations for a seventeen-day mission, so we had to eat only one partial ration per day in order to make them last. I lost five pounds.

We had a week off after the operation, so the team and I decided to see some of the country, except for the Skipper, who decided to stay behind. The rest of us walked to the nearest town called Taktagahara which was about a mile outside the base camp. There we boarded the train to Tokyo. The train system even back then was really something. The bullet trains ran around a hundred sixty miles per hour. Tokyo was over two hundred miles from where we were based, and the trip only took one hour and thirty minutes. Those things really traveled; it is no wonder they called them bullet trains. Tokyo is a very large city of about ten million with the area population totaling around thirty-five million. The form of money is the Yen. The exchange at the time I was there was three hundred fifty Yen for each American dollar. We all thought we were rich. We visited a lot of sites in Tokyo but the most interesting for me was the Ginza strip. The restraints and the nightclubs were quite a site. There were Geisha Houses on the strip as well and each of us was assigned a Geisha. She was there to please us in any way we requested (with one exception, no sex). My Geisha's name was Kayko (however, I understand they never used their real names). They have community bathing there, and it was their custom to bathe before dinner. Kayko started disrobing me and escorted me into the bath. She carefully folded my clothes and stacked them in the order they would be donned back on. Then she disrobed and got into the bath with me and started sponging me off, being very respectful. When the bath was over and after she was dressed, she helped me into a kimono, then she escorted me to a private dining area where she served me a dinner of Teriyaki steak with Rice, Rice pudding for dessert, ginseng tea, and Saki (Rice wine). All this she did in ancient ritual tradition. Kayko then moved me to a pad on the floor, where I received a massage from top to bottom, back and front; then back to the bathing area for another bathing; then she dressed me and we went back to our private dining area, where we had another cup of tea. Then she escorted me back to the main area of the house. During the entire time, she never looked me in the eye, was highly professional, always asking, if she pleased me, and never did she or any of the other Geishas with the other guys solicit sex. It was strictly and totally professional. However, there are plenty of places in Japan that offer sex in any way, shape, or form, and I frequently visited some of those places. Visiting the Geisha House was one of my most memorable experiences.

After the week was up, it was time to leave Japan and head to the Philippine Islands for survival training in the jungle, along with escape and evasion.

Subic Bay/Jail

The USS *Cavalier* was waiting at the dock when we arrived at Yokohama. It would be an eight day trip, and I was looking forward to being out at sea again. We had an uneventful trip to Subic Bay, but this time the ship would stay in port. We had liberty call that evening (Cinderella, of course), and Hoppy, Tommy, and I decided to go into town and tie one on. We drank everything from beer to champagne. Hoppy and Tommy had to carry me back to the ship. The officer on deck saw me being carried by a sailor and went off on me. I didn't mind that too much, but then he called me a *son-of-a-bitch* and I reacted by knocking him on his ass. That did not go over well, not very well at all. I was confined to the ships brig, awaiting office hours. On the next day, I had office hours, vide article 32 of the UCMJ (Uniform Code of Military Justice), where I was told what my punishment would be, or I could request a courtmartial. I thought, if I took the courtmartial and lost (a very good chance that I would), my career might be over. I took the punishment, ten days in the brig, ten days' loss of pay, a one rank deduction to CPL and extra duty for forty-five days. I was devastated, dejected, and felt like a heel. I felt I had let my team down and did not blame them if they had requested a replacement. They assured me everything was cool and not to worry but that I should have held my temper. I probably would have if I had not been drunk. Well, if I had not been inebriated, the entire event would never have happen in the first place! The entire team and my Platoon Commander, 1LT. Daniels, went to bat for me at article 32, and I believe that is why my punishment was lenient. I did not get to participate in the operation in the Philippines. After I got out of the brig, I spent the rest of the time aboard ship in the bakery shop, and on mess duty, and when we arrived back in Okinawa, I had another three weeks' extra duty and no liberty, so I could not visit the dojo.

Rank in the Marines, traditionally, is fairly slow; usually the promotion board turns you down the first time, and in some cases the second time before they grant a promotion. I was one of the lucky ones, having been promoted every time I went in front of the board. It took a year of hard work and study to receive those three stripes, and in just a few short minutes, one of them was gone; it would take me over a year to earn that stripe back, or even longer. I knew I was lucky with article 32, and I was grateful for what everyone did for me, but it sure was a bitter pill to swallow. I might add that the Officer on the deck whom I hit was reprimanded for his verbal actions against me.

Back to "The Rock"

Back on "The Rock" it was business as usual, with training, training, and more training, concentrating, and staying sharp in our jobs. By this time we were a sound fighting unit;, though we had not been in combat, everyone felt we were ready, and the important thing was that we *knew* we were ready too.

It was now the middle of July 1964 and getting close to the critical part of our tour overseas: the float phase, where the battalion was out at sea for four months. It is at this time that we would be the 911 force for the entire Southeast Asia region. When anything happens, we were the ones to get the call; if the balloon did not go up, well we could enjoy all of the ports of call; Taipei, Hong Kong, Manila, Bangkok, Singapore. I wanted to see these places, if for no other reason, than to tell my grandchildren I had been there.

August 1 was our last liberty call before we had to board ship and leave Okinawa for the second time. I was to take my black belt test at the dojo, and I was very nervous about taking the test, even thought I had practiced for it for a couple of weeks. There were three judges, Master Sakimoto and two eighth degree black belts from another dojo. The judges' decision must be unanimous in order to pass the test. Your form must be near perfect, and if you miss a Kata or any part of one, you cannot go back and correct it; they must be completed in the order laid out and in succession, each in their entirety, in order to successfully pass the test. I received two green flags (successful completion) and one red (fail). Master Sakimoto gave me the red flag. He stated that my form was not up to par, but that I had completed all six Katas correctly. Even though I did not pass the test, I was satisfied with my performance and felt I had done my very best.

Master Sakimoto

Master Sakimoto was a strict disciplinarian, never allowing anyone to get out of line in any way. He was also a perfectionist, accepting nothing but perfection in his students. He would not praise any student for trying their best or not even for being near perfect; and that was at the beginner level as well. He did not tolerate frustration, anger, pessimism, procrastination, or bad attitudes. Master Sakimoto would not ask you to leave the dojo; he told you to leave and come back when you were ready to be his student, his way; if you had to leave a third time because of any of the above negatives, you were banned and could not return to his dojo.

I learned so much from Master Sakimoto, and I am grateful for having been his student. In August 1964, I took my black belt test and passed it according to the standards in the United States and Japan, but not by Master Sakimoto's standards, and did not receive my black belt. I could have retaken the test when I returned to the United States and received my black belt, but it would not have been the same. It wasn't me I wanted to please; it was Master Sakimoto, and I had failed at that. It was okay, though; I wasn't trying to be a Master or go into the profession of teaching the martial arts; it wasn't and still isn't my cup of tea; I accomplished my mission there, and it was to defend myself when and/or if I had to. It is amazing sometimes that when you take on a task to learn one thing, in the process you learn so much more. Not only did I learn self-defense and discipline, but in the process I also learned about life. I have never forgotten Master Sakimoto's philosophy on life; I will always be grateful to this man.

CHAPTER FOUR

USS Valley Forge

The battalion boarded the buses to make the one-hour trip to Naha, the capital of Okinawa where we would board the ships taking us on the last phase here of our overseas tour. The battalion would be aboard four ships: two APAs (amphibious, personnel, and assault), USS *Cavalier* and the USS *Pickaway*; one AKA (assault, cargo ship) USS *Libra*; one LPH (landing platform helicopters) USS *Valley Forge*. Back in World War II, the big aircraft carriers needed more planes than they could carry to battle areas, so smaller carriers (jeep carriers) were built to accommodate those big carriers by holding planes in reserve. When one plane would go out of commission, the big carrier would radio back to the jeep carrier to send another plane. After World War II, the helicopter was beginning to be a very versatile tool in the arsenal, so the old jeep carriers were recommissioned as LPHs.

All Marines, when at sea (for over thirty days), are assigned duties to help the Navy out (we called it payback for carrying us around). Some of these are voluntary, some mandatory; mandatory duties, mess duty (KP), swabbing decks, message courier, etc. I always wanted to be in the bake shop; went to work at 2300 hours and was off by 0400 hours. We would bake all of the food (pastries, breads, meats, all foods that required baking) for the next day and put them in warmers. The head baker was Chief Petty Officer Harry (Cookie) Black and his assistant, Petty Officer Jimmy Jones. These guys could bake anything to perfection, every time; they would get more work out in five hours than most could in twelve. At first, I wanted to work in the bakery because of the limited hours, but after time, I really liked it. I loved working with those men. It was just the three of us and I learned a lot about cooking and baking. Cookie always said, "Time to feed my boys and it has to be special." Both of them took their work very seriously, like it was a matter of life and death; and I guess it was in one way. If an Army travels on its stomach, I don't suppose the Navy and Marine Corps are any different.

After ten days at sea, we arrived at our first port of call, Manila, Philippines. Liberty call started at 1600 hours and I decided not to go ashore, for two reasons; first, I had already been there. Five miles down the road was Subic Bay, where I lost a stripe back in March, and the other reason, I had to be back in the Bakery by 2250 hours. We were there to take on fuel and supplies so we departed the next day.

Our next port of call was Taipei, Taiwan, where we would be tied up for three days. The guys in the bake shop said they would not be going ashore until the next day, so I told the guys in my team and they decided to go with us. Both Cookie and Jones had been at all these places, and they knew where to go. The next day, at 1000 hours, liberty call went out and we hit shore; the taxis and rickshaws were on the dock to take us to town. None of us Marines had ever ridden in a rickshaw, so we decided to hail one. The people pulling those rickshaws would run at an amazing speed for over an hour at a time (sometime more), for a quarter (.25 cents), anywhere we wanted to go arriving at a destination sometime faster than a cab. We saw the sites of the city, went to a club, had a few drinks and danced with the local girls, then went back to the ship. We were out all day and it was early evening (about 2100 hours) when we arrived back at-the ship. It was a fun trip. I had a blast riding in that rickshaw, seeing the sites and the culture of the Chinese people.

The next port of call was Hong Kong. At the time I was there, Hong Kong was a British owned Colony, so the predominant language was English. I had always heard two things about Hong Kong; Thieves Market, and the taxis were Rolls Royces. I thought it was time to find out about both. The ship anchored in the harbor, so we had to take a water taxi (supplied by the Navy) to shore. When we arrived we had to exchange our money from American dollars to Hong Kong dollars at a rate of twelve to one (one being American).

Hong Kong's population at the time I was there was just over four million, making it the fourth largest city in the world. From the harbor, it looked like New York City. We had three days' liberty and we decided to make the most of it. Four of us in the team decided to rent a hotel room; we found one for $120 a night (ten dollars American) and stayed for two nights. We found some girls and hooked up with them (in more ways than one); they showed us the city, took us to Thieves Market and other places, like the night spots. While at Thieves Market (it is not a small place; it is a city within itself) I bought several items; ivory fans, an ivory chess set, a suit of clothes, and a sweater. The sweater and the suit were stolen before I got out of the market area. This is why they call it Thieves Market; before you leave the area, kids will come up from behind you and snatch the stuff; they are gone in a flash and you don't know where they went. You can get some really great things there at rock-bottom prices, but be prepared to lose it before you get out of there. After we left the market area, we hailed a cab to take us back to the hotel; and yes, it was a Rolls Royce.

On the next morning, we were awakened by a loud knock on the door. When I opened the door, this SP (Shore Patrolman) was standing there and asked, "Are you with The Valley Forge task force?" I told him that we were; he said that liberty was canceled and all personnel must return to ship, ASAP! My first thought was that someone had got into trouble or, even worse, killed, and then it hit me like a ton of bricks; we were being called back because the task force was ordered to Vietnam. Then I got that sinking feeling, like you were all alone in the world but everyone was still there. We gathered our gear and made it back to the ship as fast as we could.

When we arrived back on board, we were getting all kind of scuttlebutt; we are headed to Nam, another rumor had it, we were going back to The Rock; another was we were going to Sydney, Australia, for R and R; and another, we had to pull out of harbor because a typhoon was headed our way. The Rock and Sydney thing didn't make any sense, so it had to be the first, the last, or both. Whatever it was, none of the brass was saying anything; they probably did not know themselves. When orders come aboard ship, they are sealed and cannot be opened until past the point of no return (at a latitude and longitude marked on the outside of the orders). All the information the captain is given is to proceed to that azimuth on the outside of the sealed orders.

As it turned out, there was a typhoon and we ran right in the big middle of it. It tossed the ship around like a little toy boat on Lake Ouachita back home. The waves were estimated at over sixty feet high, which completely covered the vessel. There was no sleeping on that boat during the storm, and very little eating; and forget about going topside, unless you wanted to become shark bait. Marines have plenty of guts, but the Navy has no fear when it comes to rough seas. They continued their work like it was just another day at the office. I don't know if it was no fear or they were crazy as hell. Be that as it may, they got the job done. While in the storm, there were six more ships that joined our task force: one APA, two AKA, and three destroyers. I believe we all knew then where we were going.

We rode that typhoon out for nineteen days before we finally broke through. When we did, we received our destination, the Gulf of Tonkin, South Vietnam; however, we had no orders to hit the beach at that time.

Going Ashore

The task force floated in the (Gulf of Tonkin for twenty-one days, and then we got the call; my company was to go ashore to set up an outpost to guard the Air Base in Da Nang. We were not considered combat troops, but a peacekeeping force. We were not to go on the offensive, only return fire if fired upon. I and any member of the team did not like these terms; but the order came from President Johnson. I thought to myself, if he knew so much about combat tactics, maybe he should be here with us!

The Navy Seabees were there clearing ground for a line of fire, building fences, and stringing concertina wire, completely around the air base; our job was to protect them as well.

The battalion was scheduled to board ships for return to the United States on December 10. We went ashore in The Republic of Vietnam (RVN) on October 12. I did not believe we would be home for Christmas or New Year. We would be stuck on top of this hill, eating c-rations, trying to stay dry from the monsoons, and waiting for the VC to bring a sizable force and try to overrun us. We were going out on patrols every day, trying to draw fire from the enemy, so we could shoot back and keep them disorganized. None of us liked the orders we had; we could only return fire when fired upon. We were not to engage the enemy; we had to wait for them to engage us. It was like being pawns on a chessboard, with no knights, bishops, castles, or queen. The kink was back in Washington, DC, and we all felt he didn't give a damn! November came and went, December came and went, and we were still in the same place, turning the VC back, when they would launch an attack against us; in all, we turned back the VC eleven times during our tenure there. We received no casualties, except for "Money Bags"; he tripped on a rock and sprained his ankle. On January 9, replacements from the Army's 101st Airborne finally arrived, and we could leave. It was a happy bunch of Marines that day when we said, "*Good-bye, Vietnam*!" We left the country the next day, after our relief was briefed, and left directly for San Diego; steaming time, twenty-one days, including a two-day dock at Pearl Harbor. We did not mind that, though we could use some liberty; and liberty we had! We were all over the island, like kids in a candy store. Liberty was only for six hours, but we made the most of it.

State Side

On January 31, 1965, San Diego was on site and cheers went out all over the ship. We had finally made it. It was the longest twenty-one days I believe I had ever spent anywhere; the anticipation of getting back to the states was nerve-racking, to say the least.

Mom and Dad had gone on vacation back home to Arkansas to see the folks, so I decided to take the train back there as well. The chief wanted me to travel with him to Gary, okay, and meet his family on the reservation, so I decided to make the trip home via Oklahoma. He had called his parents at San Diego and told them he was bringing a friend home to spend one night. It was a long train ride to Oklahoma, but when we arrived, Amick's family was there to embrace him, and they welcomed me as well.

On the reservation, their traditional ceremonials were in order. All the people on the reservation turned out having a huge BBQ, Native American style. There were ceremonial dances and games of all types, all in honor of their native son (Amick). It was one of the most impressive homecomings I had ever seen; my thoughts surveyed ahead, and I wondered what my family had in store for me. There would probably be the proverbial hugs and kisses, and someone will say, "Let's have a cookout," which will not happen if someone doesn't mention it.

On the next morning, I said my goodbyes to Amick and his family, and thanked them for their hospitality. I was on my way to Benton, a place I had not seen for two years.

I called my grandfather's house, where my parents were, and told them when my train would arrive so they could pick me up. Finally the train rolled into the station and there was Mom and Dad out there, and along with them, to my surprise, were my oldest friends, Richard and Charlie. I was so excited to see them that I was in tears. Charlie heard about my homecoming and said he wouldn't miss it for the world. Richard had arrived home on leave returning from Korea and he had to come as well. Man, was this great! I could not believe all three of us were together again. The drive to my grandpa's house was only five minutes, and there were cars lined up on the street almost as far as you could see. All my aunts, uncles, and cousins were there just to see me, I thought . . . Turns out, they planned a family reunion around my homecoming. It worked out great! There was enough food to feed a battalion; everyone playing games, talking over old times, and of course there was Grandpa. Everyone seemed to be around Grandpa and me. I was the first grandchild to enter the service, and that was a big deal for him. I told him it was a bigger deal for me to be home with him, Mom, Dad, and the rest of the gang.

The reunion started to break up about four in the afternoon, so my attention went to Mom and Dad. They had to leave in four days back to California because they only had nine days' vacation. They wanted me to go back with them, but I declined; I wanted to spend more time with my two friends and Grandpa. The next day I told my grandpa that I had thirty days' leave, and that is when he told me of his vision, which I mentioned in an earlier chapter.

Later that day, Charlie came over with Richard in his new car and we went for a drive to Malvern and around the countryside, talking over old times and drinking beer. We had the best time; just being with one another was special. We spent at least two to three hours with each other for the next eight days; then, on the tenth day, my leave was cut short with a phone call as my grandfather said it would. I said my goodbyes, and Charlie and Richard drove me to the bus station, where I waved at them and they waved back until we were out of sight.

My heart felt very heavy, and it was very hard to swallow, leaving my friends so early and thinking about what Grandpa had said; he would not be here when I returned. The prediction about the phone call was accurate; would the rest be as well? It kept playing over and over in my mind; I tried to transfer my thoughts to something else, but as I closed my eyes, I would see his face, repeating those words over and over again, and I felt tears running down my cheeks, thinking, if Grandpa was right, I will never see him again, and it made me sad to think what would I do without him . . .

The trip was uneventful until the bus arrived in El Paso, Texas. Almost everyone in the bus terminal was glued to the television; some were running around to see what was going on; others were stunned and feeling numb. The train derailment was the top story! Then it hit me so hard; I became weak with emotion and started weeping bitterly. What Grandpa said to me had come to pass, and I knew that the rest of what he had envisioned would happen as well. I would never see him (Grandpa) again, and I was going back to Vietnam, and it wasn't going to be like it was before; it was going to be the most horrible experience I would ever encounter and would relive those horrors in my mind for the rest of my life.

CHAPTER FIVE

The Trip Back

The Adoption

When I arrived back at Del Mar (February 15), the battalion was very busy preparing all of the vehicles, equipment, and weapons to load onto the ships. The entire First Marine Division was to move out and they would all be in place by July. We were the first to go (the advanced party). No liberty was authorized for anyone, not even the brass; we worked around the clock until all the work was done (about six days). Then it was time to prepare ourselves for the trip and for the hornet's nest we were to face for at least the next fifteen months and possibly more. We had some idea of what to expect, only this time we were on the offensive; this time we were to hunt our little yellow-skinned brothers, find them, and kill them. None of us wanted to be back there, none of us wanted to kill or be killed, but maybe this time the odds would be in our favor. We did not know what to expect, or if for sure, we were even going back to Vietnam, for no orders had been announced; this was speculation on everyone's part; sometimes you don't need to receive orders; some times you just know by what is happening around you, and this was one of those sometimes.

After all the work was done, we were granted five days' emergency farewell leave. All the guys in my team, including the Skipper, asked if they could come home with me; they did not have family close enough to visit within the five day allotted time, but they all wanted to be around family at this time, *any family*!

When Dad came to pick me up, I told him that all the guys were coming too and to make room for everyone. The trip to my parents' house in San Clemente was only a five minute drive from Del Mar. We all piled out of the car, and Mom said, "We will find room somewhere." Dad said it was going to be tight quarters, but it will be like the Hilton, compared to some of the places we would be staying; we all agreed on that statement.

We all went out to eat at one of the local restaurants (a place called the Smorgasbord). We were all talking; Mom and Dad knew two members of the team (the chief and Hoppy) from previous visits, but did not know any of the others. As he was talking to the rest of the guys, they were on the subject about the incident at Subic Bay, when I lost my stripe. Mom or Dad did not know that I had gotten drunk and they were surprised and disappointed to find out about it; not so much about getting drunk, but not telling them the whole story. Mom and Dad bonded with all the guys and treated them like their own; they even wrote all the guys letters while overseas, telling them they loved them and were thinking of them every day. They adopted the team as I did and cared for them and were concerned for their safety; and the team adopted Mom and Dad as well. We all assured Mom and Dad we would take care of one another over there just like we have since we had been together.

While at home, we went to Disneyland, Knots Berry Farm, Hollywood, the San Diego Zoo, and I can't remember all the places we visited, and all the things we did; places we had been to before, but this time it was different; this time it was special. We made those five days like they were our last, and Mom and Dad tagged along wherever we went; they took time off to be with us, and the team talked about it among themselves for a long time after.

Five days go quickly when you don't know when or if you are going to get any more time, especially to spend like we did. I was so proud of my parents; they opened their door and their hearts to all the men in my team, and I thought this should never have to end, but, as it is said, good things do end for a time, and this one was not an exception to that statement.

Our leave was up at 1800 hours on February 27, and the next morning we pulled out of Camp Del Mar for another time, not knowing if we would see the place again; we all had hope that we would. We all had critical MOSs; if you survived a mission, you were lucky. We were a team of seven, not seven hundred, or even seventy; only seven. It was most likely that half of us, if not all of us, wouldn't be coming back, and we all feared for one another, and that made each of us feel even closer to one another. We were a band of brothers.

The Trip Back Over

As we boarded the USS *Pickaway*, I was looking to see if my parents were among the many well-wishers seeing their loved ones off. I did not see them at that time, but Tommy did, and he said, "There they are, Don!" After we were on board, we put our gear away and went up topside so we could see them again. We weren't scheduled to leave for four hours, so we received permission to go down on the pier and visit for a couple of hours. While there, my dad broke down and started crying, and that made my mother cry, which made me start crying, which made the rest of the team start crying. We had a pity party right there in front of God and everyone, right there on the pier! Everyone, including me, finally regained our composure and we were back to ourselves again. Dad asked me if I wanted them to stay in California. I told him that it wasn't up to me where they lived; it was where they wanted to live. Why he asked me that, I don't know. He had a great job and great pay and both Mom and Dad liked it out there. Why he would even think about leaving that situation was beyond me, and I told him so; and then I said, "Dad, back in Arkansas, you worked hard your entire life and had very little materially to show for it. Then you come to the west coast and things started to click for you. You would be a damn fool to walk away from what you have accomplished here."

He said, "You are right, Son, but it is so far from Arkansas."

I responded, "If you want to go back to Arkansas, go. I think it is a mistake, but you do what you think is best. Just let me know what you decide, so when I come back, I will know where you are, okay?" I really thought it was a mistake for him to even think about leaving California, when things were going well for them, unless Mom was putting the idea in his head. She always wants to be close to her dad (Grandpa). I had not told my parents what my grandpa had said to me while I was on leave, because I knew it would only upset Mom. Maybe she could sense something; you know what they say about women's intuition.

The *Pickaway* had blown her horn for a second time, which meant it was time to get aboard, so we said our goodbyes again through teary eyes, and the team and I went aboard; in the next hour, we set out to harbor and into the vast Pacific.

The trip was uneventful for the first ten days; then we hit a squall, and the ship was tossed around like it was a toy. Three days before the ship ran into the storm, our sealed orders were opened and, yes, our destination was the Republic of South Vietnam.

We were now in another typhoon, and we were informed that there were two in our path. The ship was braving the storm and taking on sixty-foot waves. Time after time the ship would rise as the waves came, then slam down on the sea; it sounded like we were hitting concrete every time. The ship cannot lie still or be in harbor when a storm hits; it could be damaged and people injured, so we continued on. The bow of the boat was splitting and Navy Seals on board were repairing her to keep from taking in so much water. The ship fought the storms for twenty-seven days before we finally ran through them. That was a rocky ride for a long time, and we were still six days away from the Gulf of Tonkin. It was supposed to be a seventeen-day trip, and after twenty-seven days, we still liked six days. The typhoons had really added to our steaming time. We had to take on fuel from tanker ships three times, because we were unable to dock into a port.

When we reached the Gulf of Tonkin, I was sure we would be going to shore right away (because of the delay), but we didn't. There were a total of eight ships that made the trip, and we floated for another two weeks. If a Marine waits long enough, he gets the word to disembark; and the word finally came to climb over the side, down the nets, and into the Peter Boats. After the first wave was assembled in the boats, they hit the beach. This group was to go forward off the beach and set up a perimeter and run patrols (four recon teams, including the "Wolf Pack" (my team), were running patrols), in protection for the rest of the troops coming later, in the second and third waves, and eventually the main body and all the equipment. There was no enemy in sight and we had an uneventful landing, thank God!

After the battalion was ashore along with two battalions of infantry and a company of Seabees, we received the order to move out.

CHAPTER SIX

Getting Reacquainted With Charlie

The Outpost

The monsoon season was going to start up again in a couple of weeks, and we would look forward to a couple of months of one front after another with constant rain and wind everywhere. We moved out to our position, about twelve clicks northwest of Da Nang, where we were to set up an outpost and monitor all incoming and outgoing traffic, to and from the Da Nang area. There were four such positions to be in place from the southwest, but my team (the "Wolf Pack") was the only outpost guarding a major road. The other three positions were there to observe and report, and to reinforce us in case we needed them.

We set up just off the road, with the Alpha and Charlie teams to our right and left flanks; the Delta team was one click south of us. There were no civilian vehicles allowed past our checkpoint traveling into Da Nang. Nothing but the military was allowed in, and it was our job to check every vehicle, and turn back any that was not authorized. Over ninety percent of vehicular traffic was military, and it was quite boring, but we could not afford to be lax and take things for granted at the outpost. There were a lot of local civilian personnel that used the road, going to and fro making a living. They would have their yokes of baskets of food and goods that they collected from wherever they worked, mostly rice paddies. Some would be on bicycles but most would be walking. All the locals were given papers of authorization to travel up and down the road; without them showing their papers to us, they could not pass. They could leave without showing their papers, but they could not return without them.

There were a lot of kids (about eight or ten) that would hang around especially in the late morning and try to sell us cokes, rice, and Banh Mi (Vietnamese Baguette or French bread); sometimes they would have Vietnamese Beer and Manila Rum. The brand of the beer was Tiger rue; we named it *Tiger piss*, because most of the time it was hot, and even when it was cold it tasted like crap. We called the manila rum just exactly what it was: Rot Gut, because it would sure enough mess you u, in more ways than one. Sometimes we would buy and sometimes we would not. There was this little girl of about nine years of age, named Mi Ling in the group; we grew to be very attached to her, and when we started buying most of our banh mi and cokes from her, the others stopped coming around. She was as cute as a bug and so polite. She sold us cokes and banh mi and took the money home to her mother. Her father and older brothers had been killed several years earlier in the war, during the French occupation.

We were to be at the outpost for one month and then be relieved by the infantry grunts. We were there to give them time for their units to get organized, and then we would leave, head north, and set up our base camp, where all the action was happening. After about two and a half weeks, the monsoons hit, along with a tropical storm, and it was a mess! It came like Noah's flood and didn't let up for about three days. Not only were we soaked, but also the tents we put up were gone; the rains hit so fast that we did not have time to protect them from washing away. Marine Reconnaissance, Special Operations groups travel light. What we had in our rucksacks is all we had; the only other cover would have to be built from what the land provided for us and our ponchos. We were on our next to last battery for our radio, and the Lima Lima (landline) we had when we got there had been knocked out by the tropical storm. If we did not get relieved on time, we would be in a fix, without communication.

All traffic had ceased, in—and outbound. The road was a dirt road, and even the six-bi's (two and a half ton trucks, for you in the Army) couldn't make it through that mess. You could not even walk without sinking down halfway to your knees; after the tropical storm left, the monsoons kept dumping rain on us and that just made things worse; that is, if it could get any worse. We also knew that this situation was what the VC waited for; this was their kind of weather When we radioed back to the HQ of our situation, we were told we would be there until further notice, and to only use the radio to communicate with the other teams in place and to call in sit raps (situation reports) to HQ every six hours instead of the one hour SOP on the Lima Lima (field telephone landline), in order to prolong the life of the batteries; they said they would send a cable crew out to fix the landline and to be prepared to live off the land because there would not be any trucks out to drop us off any c-rations.

We commenced to build our hooch out of bamboo poles, small cane sticks, brush, and elephant grass, so at least we could keep the rain off us; it would not keep us completely dry, but at least it would keep us from going dinky dowh (crazy).

After three days, we still did not have a lima lima, so the next morning, the Skipper and Hatfield went to the Alpha team to try and get a couple of men, and the four of them would try and trace the wire out to see if they could find the problem and fix it. They were gone most of the day; about 1400 hours or about our lima lima was ringing. We were able to get a disposition on chow and relief now. HQ had said no trucks were running yet, and wouldn't for at least another week. We were stuck there until our relief arrived.

We had been on thirty percent watch (two men every four hours) and continued maintaining the schedule.

We had run out of c–rations two weeks ago and were eating pineapple off a tree close by, and it was getting mighty old; at least we would not get scurvy, ha! We would also catch rainwater in our helmets to fill our canteens. We weren't starving, but a steady diet of nothing but pineapple was taking its toll on us; I swore that when we were able to get some real food, I would never eat pineapple again.

After a solid month of rain (with two to three hour breaks every two or three days), the rain stopped. On the third day, I saw a truck in the distance coming out of Da Nang; we flagged it down and asked them if they had any food or c–rations. The assistant driver said that there was a case of something in the back, and we were welcome to it. I looked in the back; there was one case of food, and I got it. Pineapple! One lousy case of pineapple! Our tree was getting low, so I thought we had better take it. When the truck came back three days later, he stopped and threw out a case of hot dogs; Hot Damn, Hot Dogs! We told the others at the other posts and they sent runners over to get their share. There were three hundred dogs in that case, and we ate every one of them in less than an hour (of course, after we shared them with the other posts, everyone only got eleven each). After about two hours, we got sick to our stomach. The hot dogs were okay; but we had been on a diet of pineapple for so long that our stomach would not tolerate an overabundance of something else. Hoppy warned us of this but we didn't listen; we did the next time!

VC activity had been all around us, for the past three weeks, and it was getting closer. We were ordered to start running ambush patrols, out about a click from our parameter, at night, to keep the VC at bay. On the fourth night, my team set in for ambush on a trail that looked like it had been used frequently. We had been set in for about two hours, and here they came; we knew there were no friendly troops in the area, so we cut loose on them. After less than a minute we ceased fire, and nine VC lay dead: seven men and two women. Three of them were some of the kids that sold us cokes and beer before the monsoons had started. I thought at first that we had made a mistake, but I was wrong. They carried weapons (AK47s), and they had North Vietnamese documents on them. It was devastating to know that we were going to have to kill kids; some of them were only thirteen or fourteen years old. The reports we received months ago were true. The North Vietnamese Army recruited people in the south (even kids) to fight for their cause by holding their relatives hostage or threatening to kill them if they did not join them. Then, my first thought was little Mi Ling; what if they got to her? What if they already had? I told the others in the team of my feelings and they were thinking this too.

What was supposed to be three weeks at the outpost turned into almost three months; we finally got word that we would be relieved by the end of the week, and we sure were glad. We would be moving to the airport for five days of rest before moving up north about fifty clicks (50 km) in the heart of VC occupied territory.

The day before we left, we saw Mi Ling coming as she had on many previous occasions, but this time she stopped about a hundred meters from the checkpoint and just stood there; she looked different, like she was in a trance, or she was scared. I started to go to her, to see what was wrong, and the skipper said no. "I saw this in Korea several times; the enemy will use these kids as bait, and when several GIs are around her, they ambush them killing her and the GIs, or they plant TNT on them and detonate it." I did not know what to do; I felt helpless, but felt I couldn't just leave her out there for the VC to blow her to bits. Two guys in the team felt the same as I did. The chief and Hays had left to recon for VC in the area. They stayed hidden in the tree line to keep from being seen. Then I heard rifle and automatic weapons going off from two different directions and we hit the ground. In less than thirty seconds, it was over. Twenty VC lay dead. The Alpha team on one side, with Amick and Chitchester on their flank, cut down on them; they did not have time to react. We found a detonating plunger that would have set off the bomb on Mi Ling's back. WD1 wire was hooked to the plunger, which was strung onto the bomb. The guys disconnected the wire, and the bomb was safely removed from Mi Ling. I took her in my arms and took her to the checkpoint area, while the Skipper and Nettleton set the bomb off from a safe distance. While we were all glad that Mi Ling and her little dog were safe, I knew that there would be a lot more like her that would not be, and I cried for them. Charlie (the VC) made his presence known to us in a very resounding way, using kids to do their dirty work for them. Oh, we got acquainted with Charlie all right, and it backfired in his face. We may have saved a little girl today, but a little bit of us, all of us, died inside. We now knew what kind of enemy we were up against; one that resorts to brutal tactics, such as the one described above, and now it was up to us as to how we would rise up and above his brutal tactics and defeat him severely; that is, if the politicians would allow us, or would they use us like pawns on a chessboard in order to reach their own political goals? Only time would tell, but at what cost?

CHAPTER SEVEN

Firebase Bravo

(The Okay Corral)

Da Nang Barracks

When the grunt unit arrived, we loaded up on the trucks and headed to the barracks at Da Nang; I don't know why they called it a barracks, for it was just a huge area of GP large tents. The conveniences were much better, though; first of all it was dry, running water; the showers, barbershop, PX, and the sleeping quarters were great. Well at least, much better than we were used to. The Skipper made the decision, after I pleaded with him, to take Mi Ling and her mother to Da Nang with us to the refugee camp there, to protect them from the VC. There they would have good food, a decent place to live and sleep, and not have to worry about being tortured or shot.

The first thing I did was to get a long hot shower and shave; and then the next thing I got was a haircut.

We had good hot meals and they really treated us well. I also had to get my feet looked after because I was getting a case of athlete's foot (Hoppy had given us all the foot powder he had at the outpost and we used it all up before we were relieved). We also DX'd (directly exchanged) some of our equipment, especially our rain gear and utilities (fatigues), boots, and socks. Then we got some very decent and much needed rest. We only had five days, so when we weren't getting briefed on our up-and-coming responsibility up north, we were soaking up some American suds (beer) and taking it easy.

On the third day, we met our RVN Commander counterpart, CPT Chu^e; he would be making the trip with us, along with his unit, forty-eight other RVN soldiers. He was the platoon commander, and he was a bear cat, very demanding of his soldiers, and kept a close watch on them; he wanted no one goldbricking. CPT Chu^e hated the VC for what they had done and were doing to his country. His mother, father, and sister had been beheaded by the VC four years earlier, because they would not join their cause; CPT Chu^e fled to the south where he joined the southern forces to fight against the north, and worked his way up through the ranks. He knew NVN (North Vietnamese) tactics, and he and his men would be a big help to us. CPT Chu^e spoke three other languages besides his native tongue, all fluently, French, Chinese, and English, and he was a well-skilled Ty Boxer, a good man to have around when the going gets tough.

Making the trip with us as well were two teams of Navy Seals; their job was to patrol the river to our flank, and they would be based out of our compound. The area where we would be was unoccupied by friendly forces and had been since the French fall in 1954. There was not a lot of intelligence in the area, except for aerial photography of NVN infiltration. We knew that the main source of infiltration to the south (at that time) was in this area, so we were in it; we would be isolated from any friendly forces for more than forty miles, until the main body of the 1st Marine Division arrived in July and August.

Our mission was to prevent infiltration of the NVN and Chi Com (North Vietnamese Regular Army and Chinese Communist support troops) from coming down from the north and through the Laotian border. We were to recon, seek out, and engage the enemy, and push him back across the borders, inflicting more damage to him than he did on us. We took this order only one way; we were expendable!

So, this was the situation, and not a very good one; but when is war ever a good situation?

This was going to be home for at least ten months, maybe longer, if we were lucky enough to hold on to it, and if we lived that long.

The OkayCorral

We left Da Nang via helicopter (Chinooks), along with three huey gunships. We sat down about ten clicks from our destination; we would be humping it the rest of the way. My team (the "Wolf Pack") would be running point; Cpt. Chu^e (pronounced Choe) and three members of his outfit, Ba`o (pronounced Baa'oh), Bi'nh (pronounced Ben), and Nha^'t (pronounced Naigh), were with us. Bao was our point man and he knew where he was going. He knew the area quite well and stayed off the main trails; the frequently used areas were sometimes booby-trapped, with Spider Traps, Malayan Gates, Dead Falls, and/or Grenades (Spider Traps are a hole in the ground that is camouflaged, and at the bottom of the hole are spikes made of bamboo cane poles, called Pongee Stakes; usually the bamboo is full of bacteria the VC has placed on it by depositing their DNA on it. A Malayan, or Swinging Gate as it is sometimes called, is a bamboo frame with pongee stakes all inside it, attached to a trip wire; when tripped, the gate swings out or down with great force. Dead Falls are a large part of tree trunks, between five and ten feet long, positioned up high with ropes or jungle vines, which when tripped comes down on top of you; most of the time, they have spikes on them too). We were in heavy brush, and Bao had to use a machete in a lot of places. He was making good progress, however, despite the terrain and heavy brush; he really knew how to use that big knife. Not only were we fighting the brush, but we also had to look for booby traps as well.

We made it to our destination around 1100 hours, about five hours after we were dropped off.

The area we were to set up our base was elevated, and we had good vision from all four sides; the only thing it needed was a clearing area and the ARVN troops took care of that with their machetes. We commenced to build bunkers and shelters with sand bags and bamboo poles, and used ponchos connected together for roofs, until we could get the Seabees out here to improve on them. After a couple of hours, the choppers brought us out concertina wire, to be strung around each of the parameters for each platoon. The first, second, third, and fourth platoons were spread out approximately 800 to 1,000 meters apart.

We nickednamed Firebase Bravo, the "OK Corral," because when we were setting up the perimeter, the VC would harass us with small arms fire, in hopes of disorganizing us (feeling us out); nearly every day and especially at night, the VC would attack us in small forces, and on a couple of occasions, launched a mortar barrage of six to eight rounds in on us. On or about the third day, Lt. Daniels ("The Cub") made the statement, "Damn! It's like the okay Corral around here!" When he said that, we started calling it the "OK Corral."

We started running missions that evening, by running local (within two clicks of our firebase) night patrols and setting up ambushes looking for the VC. We found them sometimes, and when we did, inflected heavy casualties on them. Each time I went out, I would pray that all of us would come back all in one piece. It doesn't matter how skilled you are in your job; in combat, anything can happen at any time, and it can happen so quick, sometimes it takes a moment to regain your composure, and how you respond in that moment will determine the outcome; it's fast, furious, and high adrenaline level, which can make you react. Reaction alone is not enough in a combat situation; you have only seconds to launch a counter assault in response, and this is where your training comes in. That is why we never stop training; even when you think you're perfect, you keep at it until it becomes second nature, and then you keep on doing it, because if you screw up, someone doesn't walk away, and it just might be your buddy or you.

We had the okay corral looking pretty good two weeks after we arrived, and the Seabees brought lumber, tin, and cots; they brought a dozer and cleared a good killing zone for us, more concertina wire, claymores, and plastic explosives that we could use in the tasks and missions that lay before us. Our fifty caliber machine gun arrived, along with two 81 mm mortar teams from H & S Company of the second battalion, Third Marines, and they were a welcome sight. The Seabees also cleared a landing zone site for the choppers as well. The perimeter was beefed up; fighting holes were dug and fifty percent security was in place. We were well fortified and it would be hard to penetrate our firebase. With that being said, only seventy percent of our manpower would be at the corral on any given time. The rest of us would be on patrols such as search and seek, search and destroy, sniper, and ambush missions; most missions would only be for a day or night, which was routine, and the rest would be long-range missions which would require days, sometimes a week to ten days, due to the complexity. Then there were personnel who would get sick, wounded (WIA), killed (KIA), missing, (MIA/POW), and people coming up for R and R (Rest and Relaxation leave), if and only if we could spare them being gone. Now that seventy percent could go down as much as fifty percent or below. There were one hundred four of us (100 percent strength) at the corral, including Lt. Daniels ("The Cub"), Cpt. Chu^e, twenty-four ARVN troops, eight mortar men, and six Navy Seals (there were twelve in two teams and they rotated on the river boat). Our team consisted of seven of us and three ARVN personnel, making up a total of ten, and I hoped it would remain that way. With the exception of Hoppy (our Corpsman, who carried only a .45 caliber pistol), all of us carried rifles (M14), with automatic selectors (if needed), and the M79 Grenade Launcher, and .45 caliber pistols. One man carried an M60 Machine Gun and two of the ARVN troops operated a 60 mm mortar. We had good firepower in our team, and the three ARVN troops (Bao, Bi'nh, and Nha^'t) we had with us were good. None of them minded taking point; as a matter of fact, sometimes they would argue among themselves about it, but we all rotated, with the exception of the Skipper and Hoppy. When the chief and I would go on sniper missions, our M14 rifles stayed behind and the sniper rifles were slung over our shoulder.

The Attack

It was getting close to the end of May in 1965, and it was hot (over a hundred degrees and humidity close to a hundred as well). Back then we had never heard of the word "heat index." We had been running local missions for over two weeks; the VC were nowhere in sight; not any signs of them anywhere; I didn't like it; I didn't like it at all! A mountain yard (a primitive group of people of Indian descent) hamlet about three clicks out, who were our eyes and ears, also reported no activity in the area. When we reported this to the battalion commander, he asked what we thought about the situation. The Skipper told him that he thought they were planning something; things were too quiet, and he thought a long-range mission of search and seek should be performed. Colonel Johnson (the battalion commander) agreed, but there should be some eyes in the sky, first, to see what (if anything) we were up against, so fixed wing spotter planes were ordered to patrol up around the DMZ (demilitarized zone) and on the Laotian border. Two days later, the spotters detected movement up around the southeast corner of the DMZ; how many troops and what kind of forces was unknown. Colonel Johnson notified our company commander that a long-range reconnaissance mission should be performed to see exactly what we were up against. Two teams got the call: the "Wolf Pack" and a team from Charlie Company were to depart the next morning at first light.

On the night before we were to depart, the skipper detected on starlight a large movement of troops making their way to the firebase, and the Alpha and Charlie companies reported the same. This was not the same kind of troops that we had encountered in the past; they were NVN Regulars. They carried ladders and were in multi-wave formation (estimated at five to seven hundred; three to four to one ratio odds, in their favor), with well-organized troops; we got into our fighting holes, the fifty caliber was brought up, and the mortars were ready. This was supposed to be a surprise attack on us but we beat them to the punch! One of the mortars fired two illumination rounds, while the other fired HE and WP (high explosive and white phosphorus) rounds, and at the same time the fifty started firing, and then we were all firing from our positions! There must have been close to five or six hundred of the enemy and they were coming in waves at us! As soon as they reached the concertina, they threw their ladders over the wire and tried to cross over; as fast as they came, we were shooting them, and they were stacking up on the concertina like your mother stacks pancakes on a plate! There were dead bodies all around us! We were not the only ones with mortars. They had 'em too, and they were using them! We were taking on casualties because of the mortar attack, and the four Corpsmen in the okay Corral were staying busy, trying to tend wounds! Meanwhile, over at the Alpha and Charlie Firebases, they were busy with their problems as well. The VC had broken through Alpha's parameter and were in a hand-to-hand situation! Part of the Delta firebase personnel went to reinforce Alpha. After three hours (at morning's first light), the fighting was still fierce! The Hueys were on their way to give us air support and the word was that they would be there in ten minutes. The fighting got hand to hand sporadically at the Corral (we had our bayonets fixed), and what looked like the last wave coming on us. I felt that those choppers better get here soon, or we were going to be history! We were all running low on ammo; I barely had a hundred rounds left to stand off another forty or fifty of the enemy, and the chief was running low as well! One mortar team had already been knocked out of commission and the firing tube on the other was so hot that water had to be poured onto it! Finally, the Huey gunships arrived and they started firing rockets and cutting down the enemy with the M60s they had on board! They had them on the run and continued to pursue them. It was finally over; after over four hours of fierce fighting and taking on heavy casualties, we held our position; not only the Corral but the other firebases as well.

The casualty report at the okay Corral was three dead and seventeen wounded, six critically. Among the critical was the Skipper (my team leader) and Bao, one of my ARVN troops. Bao lost his right leg from a mortar and the Skipper took a round in his chest; he would be going home to the United States, via several hospitals. Hays (Lover Boy) received stitches from being bayoneted and returned to duty in two days. The rest of the team didn't get a scratch; they were just tired and scared as hell!

Firebase Alpha got hit the hardest, twenty-six dead and forty-three wounded, while Firebase Charlie had fourteen dead and eighteen wounded; Firebase Delta was not hit, but half of the personnel from Delta reinforced Alpha to prevent them from being overrun. Throughout the Company, we had forty-five dead and seventy-eight wounded. The body count of the enemy dead was 266, and I don't know how many were wounded, but it was a lot more of them than there was of us!

The med evac choppers had started to arrive to take our dead and critically injured to the hospital; the injured went first, then our dead. When I helped put the Skipper on that chopper, I did not know if he was going to make it or not. He was really bad off; the corpsmen had done what they could for all the guys, but a sucking chest wound; well, that was bad.

When you hear about someone getting killed, or critically wounded, or dying, you say "Oh, I'm sorry to hear about it, that's too bad, or what a shame"; but when it's your own, it's a different story and your feelings change. All of a sudden, you realize life for you or anyone of us could be over in an instant. All of us in the platoon were like brothers; hell . . . we *were* brothers, and it hurts, it hurts like hell when your brother falls! What's even harder to take is when you can't even recognize him, because he is all mangled up from being hit by shrapnel or the whole front or back of his body is blown to bits, and he is lying in more than one place! *Yes, it hurts*! It cuts deep, and the first thing that comes to your mind is to do something to help them, all of them, but you can't. There you are: "The big bad Marine" can do anything, fight off a force five times his size . . . but can't even save your friends, your buddies, your brothers! Why! Why does this have to happen! Why do we have to have this stupid war . . . Any war for that matter! Why weren't we taught how to handle this situation in Boot Camp (we were taught everything else)!

Then my thoughts turned to revenge. "I'll kill every one of those bastards . . . even if it takes me the rest of my life! I was mad (we all were); good and mad!"

Then reality hit me; our buddies are gone, and we have to deal with it. We have to pick up the pieces on the battlefield, and of the battle in our hearts and minds, and deal with it! Deal with it, with honor! That's what our fallen brothers did! They gave the supreme sacrifice! The least we can do is honor that sacrifice. We had just attained a great victory; a victory against four to one odds. Their deaths were not in vain. As I was helping put the Skipper on the med evac chopper, he was struggling to breathe, and I kept telling him to hang on and that he was going to be all right. "You are going home, Skip!" I told him half-teary-eyed and with as much of a smile I could muster. With all of his strength, he raised his hand and gave me a thumbs up, and whispered to me, "Bring 'em home, Skipper!" At that time I was ordered off the chopper. When S.Sgt. White said to me, "Bring 'em home, Skipper," those words echoed in my mind, and the gesture of thumbs up played out over and over in my mind. I had big shoes to fill, and it seemed like for a moment that I had no idea on how to go about doing it. Feeling all alone and helpless, I remember the conversation the Skipper and I had a few months back on this exact, possible situation; "Don, if I should happen to go down, do not make decisions for the team the way you think I would. Have faith in your training, have faith in yourself, because with your strong will and grit, you are the only one that can do it! Don't ever underestimate yourself, and don't ever underestimate your subordinates, and never underestimate the power of the enemy!" Then I started to feel sorry for myself, at what lay before me, and it was then that I recalled what one of my instructors in Recon said, "I have never seen a wild thing feel sorry for itself; a small bird will freeze to death on a tree branch, and fall to the ground, without ever in its entire life feeling sorry for itself." At that moment, I knelt down on my knees, and I prayed. I got up not feeling sorry for myself that day, stronger, more determined, and with the help of Almighty God to do everything I could not to lose any more of my brothers! Semper Fi!

Back to Business (Recon of Operation Starlite)

After we said good-bye to our fallen brothers, policed up, and refortified the Corral, it was time to get back into the war. The long-range mission was still on but would go off three days late.

After I was officially appointed team leader, I was given back my rank of Sergeant by battlefield promotion, and the "Wolf Pack" was back in business to do what we were trained to do; but, instead of going North, we were to go to the South, where we believed the troops that attacked us had come from, based on Army Intel. However, this was a search and seek mission, and we would be gone for an estimated time of ten to fourteen days. During the time of the mission, we were not to break fire silence (can't fire weapons), and we were to have complete radio silence.

If we were detected by the enemy, the mission would be aborted; then fire silence would be broken, and radio silence would also be broken to call in air support. We were there strictly to observe and report back.

Hoppy was not to make the trip with us, on any long-range missions or sniper missions either. He was too valuable to us to risk him. We were all trained in advanced battle first aid; Hoppy saw to that.

The Wolf Pack left out at 0300 hours of the morning (I don't know what day it was; in a combat zone, you lose track of what day it is, unless someone knows and reminds you), headed for the Central coastal area in the Quagh Ngai Province, a familiar route the NVN used to infiltrate to the South and North. I decided to take a route through the jungle in heavy canopy, at the advice of Sgt. Nha^`t, one of our ARVN counterparts, who also took the point. We had twelve days of LRMRs (Long-Range Mission Rations) of beef and rice, and chicken and rice. They were dehydrated, and each bag was good for three meals. The rations could be eaten right out of the bag, and also with hot or cold water to soften it up. Either way they were nourishing and filling; on LRMs (Long-Range Missions), we ate a maximum of twice a day. If water was used in the rations, you ate what you wanted, squeezed the water out of the remaining ration, sealed the bag up, and it would go back into a dehydrated state; this could be done four times per bag, before it would start to go bad. We carried these rations for several reasons:; they were healthy; they did not make noise; a little goes a long way; and they were a rice base, the same staple our enemy ate; therefore, our body odor would be the same as his, causing less chances of being detected.

Our first encounter of the jungles of Nam was scary. You couldn't see very well for all the vegetation, and with a heavy canopy (fifty to a hundred, sometimes a hundred and fifty feet high, the light is subdued, and it is like you are in twilight). There are spiders of all kinds, tarantulas, large rats, and snakes: the Bamboo, the Boa, the Python, the Cobra, and the Crete, to mention a few. There were also mosquitoes as big as horse flies, and leaches. Between the mosquitoes and the leaches, it is a wonder if you had any blood left in you after a mission. The mosquito repellent worked well for a while, but there was nothing for the leaches. They get all over you, your legs, your groin, all over your body! There were three ways to get them off; pull them off, which made a large open wound that would probably get infected; burn them off, where you run the risk of burning yourself and it getting infected also, or pour salt on the critter. This not only made the leach turn loose, but it also purified the opening that it made when it attached itself, having less chance of getting infection. It was normal to get fifteen to twenty leaches on you in a twenty-four period while in the jungle.

Earlier I talked about Primitive Booby traps. They were found mainly in the jungle setting, so you had to constantly be on the lookout for these as well: The Swinging Gate, Dead Fall, Pongee Traps, and

Spider Traps. All of these weapons were not only deadly but took their toll psychologically as well, if you saw one of your buddyies fall victim to one of them; so in most of the areas of the jungle, it was slow-moving, because of being on the constant lookout for these traps. If one man should fall victim to one, it meant two men were out of commission; one man had to stay behind with the wounded man until help arrived. This is why two teams were sent out. If one team had to abort, the mission fell to the other team.

Contingency plans (a plan "B" and plan "C") were made in order to complete the mission. We called them the primary, secondary, and contingency plans. If all failed, the mission was aborted and you got the hell out of the area the best way you could, as fast as you could!

When traveling in the jungle on a long range or sniper mission, you have to travel quietly and as fast as you can; the longer it takes, the percentages on being detected go up. Three to five clicks (kilometers) per hour is the average. We traveled both day and night, with a map and compass to get to our destination in a timely manner. We had approximately sixty miles to our destination, about ninety-nine clicks; I wanted to make the trip in two days: forty-five the first day, and fifteen the second. This would give us time to plan our recon while we still had daylight. We made it to our destination before noon of the second day. We had left the jungle and were on a slightly elevated area within about four hundred meters from enemy movement and activity. We were in a good place; we could see from about a span of about 240 degrees. We were in the Quan Ngai Province and close to the coast. I looked for sentries through my field glasses and did not see any, but that did not mean they weren't there. Those little yellow people had a way of concealing themselves. I sent Sgt. Nha^'t and Sgt. Bi`nh down to take a closer look, while Nettleton and Hays went down to flank them.

Nha^'t and Bi`nh were back in about forty minutes, while Nettles and Hays took a little longer. Sentries were posted at about every sixty meters around their parameter; Hays and Nettleton detected a force of the company size NVN, Hard Core Regular Troops (hard core, meaning the best they have), and it looked like they were getting ready to move out.

We decided to get a little closer to the activity, by infiltrating past their sentries to see what kind of fortifications, weapons, where their gun emplacements were, what kind of facilities they had, and approximately how many troops were there. Was it a base camp or was it just a gathering place to possibly move out to another area? All these questions had to be answered, and the reports had to be accurate, in order to plan a future invasion. The Intel we needed to collect would take two, possibly three days. We moved back to our safe haven, and later when night fell, would see what starlight, star bright would tell us.

When night fell, I turned on the Starlight night scope to scan the area and possibly go down and take a closer look at what we needed to know. Hays, Sleeper, Nettleton, and I jumped off at 2100 hours and were to return at 0400 hours. We started down to get inside their parameter and get a mental picture of their positions and to see how well fortified they were (if they were dug in, it meant they planned on staying a while, and if not, they were just passing through). They had small fires going in various places through their encampment. They did not seem concerned about concealing themselves; perhaps they did not think any Americans were anywhere around for miles, so they didn't think they needed light discipline. They were lax and doing what most military units do in a garrison area; and that is what it was. It was a large NVN base camp. It had not been there very long, but long enough for them to build hooches (we counted fifty completed hooches capable of housing twenty-five to thirty men each, and mud foundations for about twenty more), for barracks, and a large building that looked like where a headquarters and possibly a dispensary would be. Their fighting holes were deep and could house several people, and they were about fifteen to twenty meters apart. The estimated body count within the base camp was approximately 800-1000, and I believe more was on the way. They had two large five-inch artillery guns (looked like twenty millimeter), twelve mortar emplacements, and one missile stack. On the northeast side of the compound was a place cleared for what might be a motor pool, as there were ten vehicles in the area, and off to the left side of the motor pool area was a small hooch with antennas, their communications source. This was a well sophisticated camp, and they were there to stay for a while. With all the buildings in place, the large area for vehicles, the gun emplacements, and other well fortified areas; it meant a regimental, possibly larger potential force! It meant that they were there to defend the area, in order to continue their infiltration in three directions, north, south, and west!

We were inside the compound from 2100 hours until 0400 hours and were totally undetected. We made our way back to the safe haven and discussed what we observed. The Company size NVN detailed on the trail had moved out earlier that evening, and I knew that we did not have the three days to recon the area thoroughly (we had enough information, anyway), if we were to get back in time to report of the NVN on the march.

We moved out at first light, taking an alternate route to our extraction point, ten clicks out. There we could break radio silence and request extraction as soon as we could secure a safe landing zone.

While waiting for our extraction, we mapped out our observations in detail for the after action report. The trip back was a relief; I had brought my men back safely.

In the after action session of our mission, I was asked by the battalion commander what my thoughts were on the situation down south; I made the statement, "Whoever controls that area has the advantage and the largest network of infiltration in three directions. With what they have in that area, and more troops coming, they are determined to hold on to that piece of real estate, and we have to be more determined than them to take it from them!"

The search and seek mission our team performed led to the first major operation of the American Military in South Vietnam: Operation Starlite! Members of the 1st Battalion 1st Marines and 2nd Battalion 3rd Marines, along with the 1st Marine Air Wing, attacked the enemy base camp on August 18, 1965, and on August 21 declared the area secure. The Marine Infantry force killed over 700 (confirmed) of the enemy and captured over two hundred. In every battle, there is always a price to pay. The Marine Infantry lost 242, and they will always be immortally remembered; Semper Fi!

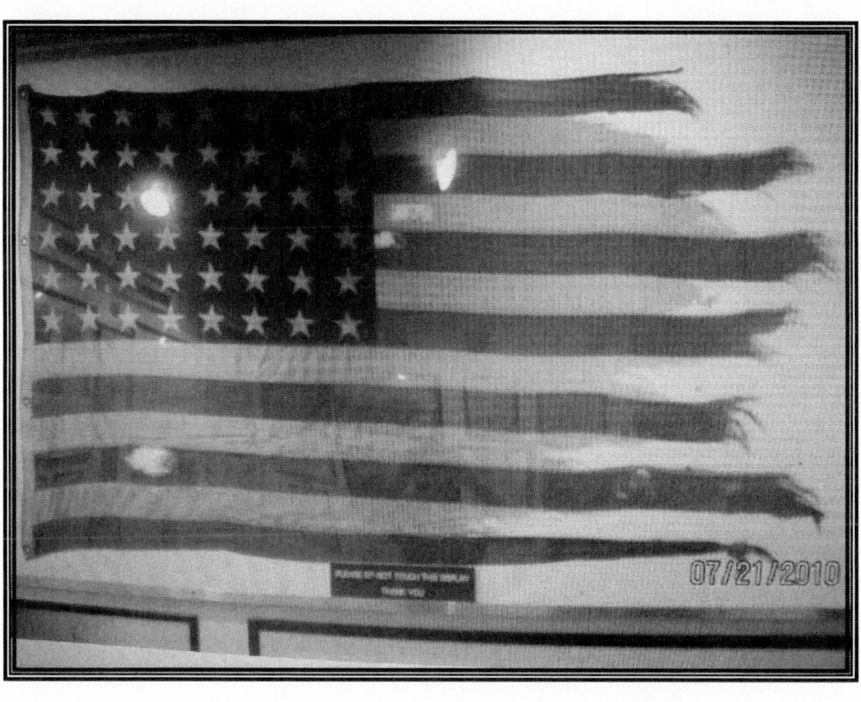
07/21/2010

The wolf pack just finishing up on search and seek mission. Awaiting extraction

I am in the middle shooting an azimuth for the recon on Operation Texas. We were getting ready to leave later in the evening

Overlooking the area from he Ok Corral

Don Reeves at 18 years.

At Subic Bay, Philippines. from left to right:
Nettleton, Hoppy, Myself.

The mopping up of Operation Texas

Myself and the team at check point Bravo, in
Quang Ngai Province during Operation Utah.

Myself on the right, with Cpt. Chu^e

A recent photo of myself and the Pretty Lady

Our Children and grandchildren
Call us Nana and Papa

Nana and Papa in front of the flag.

From left to right; Charlie, myself and Richard Life long friend.
Taken unexpectedly, Sept. 1995.

Sylvia (The Pretty Lady) and me, April, 2011

Don at, The OK Corral, in Vietnam, Sept. 1996

Don and the 'Wolf Pack' returning from mission.
The rest of the team are in front of me. Early in the year, 1966

Don pointing at the terrain in the background.
The mountain back then was known as, 'Ole Smokey'.
A part of Camp Pendleton, CA, I will never forget.
Picture taken, August, 1963

Graduation from Marine Corps Boot Camp.
July, 1963

Mi Ling; the little girl that would sell us beverages
And Vietnamese cuisine, (mostly, rice and bread).
We also save her and her mother from a horrible death.
Picture taken in (?), Feb, 1965

Lt. Daniels, AKA, 'The Cub'. This picture was taken a day or two
After the VC made their first attempt to
overrun us. They almost succeeded.
Taken May, 1965?

The pearl river up north close to the DMZ in Quang Tri Province
After our marathon run in Jan. 1966

Don, standing left. Checking mortar emplacement at the 'OK Corral. Apr 65

CHAPTER EIGHT

You Lucky Dog

Buster was a dog we adopted that just showed up one day. He was a Heinz 57 and really smart. I don't know if he had been trained or the war had sharpened his senses, perhaps a little of both. He could hear anyone coming from a mile off and could distinguish friend from foe. We learned by his actions and his growl who they were; for instance, from a very soft low growl, with the showing of teeth, and hair standing up on his back, we learned that the enemy was near, and a low soft growl with no teeth was friendly, but he did not know them, and a wag of the tail would usually be one of us. His instinct never failed us. When one of us was on watch, and if we dosed off, he would start licking our face to wake us up, and would stand watch with us, like he was in charge; and maybe he was, in a way. He became our best friend, because he would look at us, in a way, as if to say, trust me, I'll get you through this; and we did trust him.

The lieutenant wanted Buster gone and he did run him off once, but he came back the next day. He came right back to our team! We fixed up a place for him to hide inside our hooch; we dug a hole about eighteen inches deep under my cot, and allowed my blanket to drape low over the side, so his hideaway could not be seen. We were afraid the lieutenant might shoot him, and if that happened, it would piss me off, and there is no telling what I would have done to the lieutenant if he pissed me off!

One night, the lieutenant was making rounds and found Buster with Nettleton and me in our fighting hole out on the parameter. Buster was giving us the sign that the VC were in close; I was using the starlight scope on my Sniper Rifle to see if I could locate them. The lieutenant blurted out, I thought I told you people to get rid of that dog! Nettleton reached up and grabbed the lieutenant by the chest of his shirt and pulled him into the fighting hole; just as he was pushing the lieutenant in the hole, the VC cut loose with rifle fire, hitting Nettleton in the arm! In the meantime, I had located our foes and was directing my fire at them with the M-60, and at the same time the 81s (mortars) fired illumination flares! The lieutenant was putting a battle bandage on Nettleton's flesh wound on his arm! About that time, Buster jumped out of the fighting hole and took off toward the enemy, running around in circles like a crazy dog; he would get out of the line of fire for a couple of minutes, then run back toward the VC, and do it again! He even ran into their skirmish, just barking up a storm! It took us a couple of minutes to see what Buster was doing, but we finally figured it out; well, the lieutenant did. Buster was distracting them, breaking their concentration, and therefore they were no longer organized! They became a mob; most retreated and the rest of them were killed or captured (about 40 VC killed, and eight captured), with no casualties on our side, thanks to Buster. We were sure that Buster had been killed in the crossfire, but we called for him anyway; B U S T E R, *come*! And he came without a scratch on him! He was tired, that's all. The lieutenant patted him on the head and said to him, "You Crazy, Wonderful, Lucky Dog; thanks, Buster!" The lieutenant looked at Nettleton and said, "Thanks for saving my life, Marine!" Nettleton said, "Don't thank me; thank Buster! Had it not been for him warning us, we might not have known they were so close to us." The lieutenant again petted Buster on the head and said, "Thanks again, Buster; you are one special canine!" The lieutenant looked at Nettleton again and said,

"You better have Hoppy take a look at that arm, Marine, and tell him to brush up on his veterinary medicine."

Again, Nettleton's wound was a flesh wound, four stitches (without anesthetic), and good as new. As for me, I was spared again, thanks to *God* and Buster. The thought ran through my mind, "Was Buster just another mutt, or was he one of *God*'s angels sent to us to see us through all this mess." I prefer to believe the latter, because like the lieutenant said, "He was one special canine!"

After that incident, Buster not only would stay with the lieutenant's blessing, but he would help us out on our local housekeeping patrols. He proved to be very valuable, not only in locating the VC, but was also able to detect booby traps the enemy had set for us. We learned to trust him, and we made him an honorary sergeant. When we would send a detail in for supplies, we would have them get Buster some dog food.

The battalion commander got wind of Buster and at first had the same attitude as the lieutenant had, but soon changed his mind after he saw Buster in action on a patrol. I believe his exact quote was, "Very smart dog . . . glad he's on our side! Best Marine I've got!"

Operation Wolf Pack I (Roman numeral one)

Wolf Pack is the code word (and our platoon's nickname) we used for our sniper missions. The chief and I moved out aboard choppers at 0200 hours of the morning, about a week after Starlite ended. Our destination was the northeast corner of South Vietnam, near the Laotian border, close to the DMZ (demilitarized zone). We repelled out of the chopper at 0330 hours fifteen clicks (a little over nine miles) from our destination. We used our map and compass and shot an azimuth to where we were going and shoved off. There was a well fortified Gorilla Base Camp located 1500 meters from the destination. One of the high-ranking NVA (North Vietnam Army) generals was to visit that site, within three days, according to Intel; our mission was to take out that general!

Once we were out of the chopper, we donned our ghillie suits (camo gear snipers use) and camouflaged our face and hands and shoved off. The jungle was very dense in places and was slow-moving for a while. We detected several booby traps along the way, but nothing we could not handle. We met up with our mountain yard contact, about five clicks out, who took us on into our destination. There we waited; one day; two days; three days. We thought the general was not coming, but decided to give it one more day. On the morning of the fourth day, a car drove into the compound. It was him. I confirmed the range (distance of the shot) with the chief: 1,760 meters. When the general exited the automobile, he was surrounded by heavy security, and I didn't have a shot. I followed him as they walked to the hooch; some of the security force had to give way to the general as he entered the door. When that happened, I had only a second of opportunity and took the shot. A head shot! Exactly where I had aimed! The general went down with only part of his head intact! It was time to get the hell out of there! Immediately, the chief got on the radio and called for our extraction to the primary point, five clicks away. The VC would be on us quickly, so we had to hurry; we already had a 1,500 meter advantage on them! The chopper was there before we were; the pilot was instructed to circle only three minutes and then go to the secondary extraction point. We made it just in time, for when I popped the green smoke grenade so he could locate us, he was in the process of leaving! We boarded the chopper and headed back to the okay Corral. Operation Wolf Pack I was over and the mission accomplished! One shot, one kill! Semper Fi!

Operation Wolf Pack II

September of 1965 brought us to a place called Hue (pronounced Whay). Riots had broken out in that beautiful city of gorgeous white marble buildings, with its majestic Churches and Temples, between students which spilled over into the Catholic and Buddhist believers

(It wasn't the first time it happened in that city; it happened in 1963 also). It was terrible! Buddhist women were setting themselves on fire in protest against the Catholics! Bottles filled with gas were thrown into buildings and churches! Local fire and police personnel had lost control of the situation and were running for their lives!

The 1st Bn. 1st Marines of the 1st Marine Division were called up to restore order and save this city and its people. Twenty-four snipers, including myself, were to take up positions on rooftops of buildings scattered around town and shoot anyone putting our troops in harm's way! We were there also to make sure the VC did not take advantage of the situation. My sights were on the protesters; they were trying to throw gas bombs at our troops, and my orders were to shoot them before they did it! This was not a task I relished. I had nightmares for years of those people in my sights and seeing them fall to the ground! Those visions are instilled in my memory today! I shot two women who set themselves on fire! I did it because I did not want to see them suffer that kind of death! I wish it had been just a bad, horrible dream! But it wasn't; sometimes when I reflect back, I try to convince myself that it was a dream! But I can't! What a horrible site! Blood in the streets, fire everywhere, dead bodies lying all around, and a beautiful city left mostly in ruins! There were more than seven hundred townspeople who died in those riots; and over fifty Marines died, with over two-hundred wounded.

It is different when the people you have in your sights and have to kill are *not* the enemy! Your heart has an overload of burden on it! I had tears in my eyes mostly on this mission! Almost all of us did! I personally had to shoot twenty-two people, and every one of their faces is instilled in my memory! It was either shoot them or allow the Marines on the ground to get killed, and I wasn't about to allow that to happen!

R and R (Rest and Relaxation)

When we got back to the okay Corral in mid-September, it was time for us to rotate back to the air base at Da Nang for forty-five days.

R & R Delta Company would be taking over the okay Corral in our absence.

We were all looking forward to getting back to the rear area for a change, and I believe Buster was too. It had been over five months since our rotation back to Da Nang, and we were getting a little on edge, especially after Hue.

The first thing I did once I settled in was to go to the barbershop for a haircut, and after the haircut, then to the PX for supplies. I didn't have much money, only about forty dollars; I was having all my pay sent to my checking account back home. I was receiving ten dollars a month; I thought, since I didn't have any place to spend it, there wasn't any point carrying it around. The amount I had on me was more than enough for what I had to do.

I went to the Marine clothing store to DX (directly exchange) my uniforms and other garments as they were getting pretty ragged after being in the bush for so long. Direct exchange means you exchange your old clothes for new ones (boots, socks, undergarments, covers/caps, uniforms; anything Uncle Sam issued to you. We were all in bad need of everything).

After all the priorities had been taken care of, the team pooled our money and bought a couple of cases of beer, and we went back to our tent barracks and started playing spades (a card game) and did some serious drinking! After about two hours, the chief and I were elected to go on another beer run. The beer sure did taste good, but beside the beer, it was good seeing all the guys smiling and enjoying themselves again. Now don't take it wrong; each of us liked our work, but the killing fields had started to get the better of us, and we needed this break!

On the next day, we spent most of our time at the dental clinic, getting our teeth cleaned and cavities filled; we did manage to get a couple of games of spades in here and there.

That night, we took in a movie at the compound where the Marine Air Wing was housed; the name of the movie was, "No Man is an Island." That movie (a true story) became my favorite, and still is to this day. I suppose I identify with the main character (George Tweed, USN), who was all alone on the island of Guam during World War II, running from the Japanese for a period of more than eighteen months before being rescued by the Navy. Many of the islanders lost their lives helping him; quite a story! As I watched the movie, I thought of how many of the South Vietnamese had helped us. They had all risked their lives for us; some made it, most didn't!

The rest of our R and R was just lying around relaxing and taking it easy with the exception of a daily two mile morning run to keep in shape.

CHAPTER NINE

The Correspondent

We arrived back at the Corral during the latter part of October 1965 and were introduced to a news correspondent from one of the major news agencies. He was a well-known, major field agent at that time and known and respected for his non-biased reporting of situations around the world, regardless of how he felt about the subject at hand. I cannot use his real name in this writing, because I wasn't able to get permission, so we will call him John Smith.

John had a lot of questions for us; what do we think about the war? should we be here? do we miss being home? what is it like being on a patrol, or an ambush, and are they really necessary? why do we do what we do? how do we feel about the demonstrations against the war back home? We answered his questions, and when the subject of, what's it like being on patrol? I said, "Mr. Smith, since you are so anxious to know, why don't you come with us tomorrow morning at first light; I'll clear it with the battalion commander, if you would like, sir." Mr. Smith replied, Yes, Sergeant, "I think I'd like that!" The "Stockbroker" (now L/CPL Hatfield) said, "You won't like it very much if we run into Charlie; no sir, you won't like it at all!"

The next morning brought us to a muster at CCP (Company Command Post). I was instructed by "The Cub" (Lt. Daniels) to protect our visitor, but also to allow him to do his job. I told him that we would do our best, and with that exchange we left the compound and on patrol.

We had been out for about two hours when we heard AK47s; one of the rounds hit Sgt. Nha^` t, one of our ARVN counterparts. Hoppy was on him quickly. John Smith's cameraman had his camera rolling; Cpl Bi'nh stayed behind to protect Hoppy and our wounded man, while the rest of us engaged Charlie! Chief, Hays, and Little (our replacement, when the Skipper went down) circled around to the left to form an echelon assault on the enemy, while Nettleton, Hatfield, and I laid down a base of fire! We had them pinned down with our fire superiority, and when Chief's group was in position, we rushed them from both sides! With the M-60 machine gun, M-60 grenade launcher, and the rest of our small arms fire, they didn't have a chance! The ones who were still alive broke and tried to make it across the rice paddy, but we cut them down! It was over in about five minutes with eighteen VC lying dead! Mr. Smith's cameraman got most of the skirmish on film. Hatfield said, "We should have let Buster come! We may not have gotten anyone shot, if we had!" I spoke up and said, "From now on, Buster comes on all local patrols!" "Who is Buster," Smith asked? The chief said, "Oh, you got to meet Buster! You have to do a story on him for the folks back home! He is the smartest, fastest, and the baddest Marine in the Corps!"

Hoppy had stopped the bleeding on Sgt. Nha^`t's leg and had a battle bandage on the wound. We carried him to an open area where we called for an emergency med evac. After the chopper left, we secured the mission and returned to the okay Corral, where Buster greeted us the way he always did, by running to us with happy accolades of jumping and going to each of us and licking us on the hand!

After getting settled in our hooch, putting on dry socks due to the monsoons, and eating chow, our tag along correspondent asked, "Now, about this guy, Buster?" Nettleton spoke up and said, "There he is, lying at your feet; ask him how he feels about the VC." Mr. Smith exclaimed, "Buster is a *dog*! Well, what about it, Buster. How do you feel about the VC?" Buster commented with a mean growl and showing of his teeth! "How do you like Americans?" John Smith asked. Buster reacted with a gentle whine, and offered his paw to the correspondent in friendship! After Smith took Buster's paw in his, John's cameraman said, "I have to get this film to the AP (Associated Press); this is great footage!" Mr. Smith said, "Not just yet! Oh, we're going to definitely use this footage, but I want more! I want to see what this dog does, that makes him so special to these Marines that they consider him their equal!" I told John Smith that under no uncertain terms was he going back out with us and that I wasn't about to take the risk of him getting hurt or worse on my watch. He told us, it is what he does for a living; go where the story is, do what has to be done, and this is the story I want now! I consented reluctantly cleared it with the Commander for Smith to come along with us on our next rotation, which would be in three days: November 10, 1965. The Marine Corps birthday!

On the morning of the tenth, it had stopped raining for a change, and it looked as though the sun was going to shine, unusual in the peak of the monsoon season. I should have seen this sign as a warning of bad things to come, but other matters were on my mind (protecting my men, and a war correspondent; the VC also crossed my mind). When we left out on patrol, something didn't feel right. A fighting man in a combat zone develops a sixth sense about him when things are about to go wrong, and I sensed it; it was strong, very strong! I felt the other guys felt as I did, but none of us made known of our feelings to each other. I told the team to be extremely aware of everyone and everything.

Our ARVN counterparts were Capt. Chu^e and Cpl. Bi'nh. With the captain with us, he had the rank and was in charge of the patrol (we all had complete confidence in the captain and his men). Cpl. Bi'nh was point, and Buster was with him. The chief was behind the point and Capt. Chu^e behind the chief. The Stockbroker, Little, Hoppy, John Smith and his cameraman, and I were in the middle of the column, while Hayes and Nettleton had our back.

We were about four clicks into our mission, and in the Happy Valley area, where eleven years earlier the French were all but wiped out, when Buster had stopped and was looking cautious and then went down on all fours (his sign that there was danger ahead). Cpl. Bi'nh saw that it was a Malayan Gate and tripped it. It swung to the side with a force so great that it shuck the ground around us! Cpl. Bi'nh motioned all clear, but Buster remained in his position and growled as if to say, all is not clear! A closer look at the situation led to Bi'nh noticing a trip wire eight or ten feet up from the gate he had tripped! Capt. Chu^e signaled for Nettleton to take a look at the booby trap. It was one that could not be disarmed in a timely manner, and setting it off would give away our position! Going around it might get us detected and make us vulnerable to a negative situation, not to mention the possibility of the VC expecting us, diverting, and planting another trap. Nettleton, being a demolitions expert, carried white string in his rucksack; so he tied white string streamers (three or four) very carefully on the trip wire, so everyone would know where to look and avoid the wire, and we continued on. Cpl Bi'nh carried Buster over the wire, and Buster was okay.

We went another click or so and had to cross a rice paddy when all hell broke loose! Carbines and AK47s along with a .50 caliber rang out; we hit the deck and started returning fire! Cpl. Bi'nh was dead, and the chief was hit! I told The Stockbroker to get on the radio, and call for close air support, and a Med. Evac., situation desperate! They had us pinned down and nowhere to go! We were returning fire, and I was shooting grenades with my grenade launcher. If you are wondering what Smith and his cameraman were doing, I didn't really know; I was a trifle busy, directing fire, calling in med. Evac., and besides, I told them to keep their damn heads down! We needed to get at the VC from two sides, but the fire was so intense that we could not move around much without getting shot! I told Stockbroker to radio our assigned Seal team for back up! Now, PFC Little had been hit too! They were really bearing down on us, and I thought, this was it! It's just a matter of time before one of those rounds gets me! Just as I was thinking about buying the farm, I heard a loud scream and saw that the correspondent, John Smith, was shot in the leg and was bleeding profusely! Hoppy was busy with Little, so I took his belt off and used it for a tourniquet to slow the bleeding, to buy him some time, and to allow Hoppy to work on PFC John Little some more!

The Huey attack choppers arrived and started firing rockets and spraying M-60 rounds into their positions! Almost immediately, they started to disperse, carrying their wounded with them! The Hueys stayed after them for a few minutes. One of the Hueys stayed behind to help us secure a landing zone for the medical evacuation Chopper! The Med Chopper arrived about five minutes after the Hueys' assault on the VC, but the landing zone was about two hundred meters from where I was! I took off with John Smith in a fireman carry, while the other four guys carried the other wounded. The VC had come together somewhat and were firing at me and everyone else! The adrenaline in me was in full charge! I had no idea I was being shot at while running with Smith on my back! About fifty meters from the Chopper, I felt a burning in my hip! When I made it to the Med Chopper and put Smith inside, I remember falling to the ground! My right hip had given way to pain! Hoppy arrived with Little and put me on the Chopper, too. It wasn't until then that I realized I had been hit myself! I called out to Nettles to take care of Buster and the other three guys! Oh man! This is just great! I got half my team shot up, and a war correspondent! Make for a nice courtmartial! My concern wasn't for myself, though; it was for Little. His wounds were really bad. His left arm was almost gone and was losing a lot of blood. I kept talking to him to hang on, that everything was going to be all right. He was asking if Buster made it through. While I didn't know the answer to that question, I told him, "Yea, you know Buster! He is indestructible; now quit talking and enjoy the ride." He was definitely going home; the war for him was over, and if he lived through this ordeal, he would have something to tell his grandchildren! John Smith, on the other hand, had settled down and was out of shock, talking into his microphone while his cameraman was filming him and all of us. The chief was lucky! I've never seen anyone get shot where the bullet did not penetrate the skin! The round went through his caviler vest, through his shirt, and stopped! I took the round out and said, "Here you go, Chief, there's a souvenir for you!" The force of the round did break his collarbone, though, and he would be in the hospital for a while. My wound was minimal as well. What I thought was a bullet was pieces of fragments from a grenade, and I would be in the hospital for a couple of weeks and back to duty, I hoped!

We got hurt that day; half the team went down. However, with the help of the two Huey gunships and our backup support from the Navy Seal team, which lost two men as well, the VC were rendered helpless! There was still an unanswered question that weighed heavy on all our minds; Buster! That dog had saved our lives more than once since he had come to us with his impeccable instinct, smartness, loyalty, and love! However, I had faith in the remaining team members on the ground that they would take care of him and get word to us, whatever his fate was. We hoped he was all right.

The After Action

Tommy Nettleton showed up three days later on supply detail. He told the lieutenant that he wanted to visit with us while in Da Nang. He gave us the scoop on the after action report from our last patrol. Buster was found in the rice paddy, half buried in the mud. He had shrapnel in his left hind quarter and was going to be all right. Hoppy used a probe and dug out most of the fragments. He's hopping around but okay. It was a relief to know that he was still with us!

PFC Little was stabilized and had been airlifted to a hospital in Japan for surgery., Then he would be flown to a VA hospital in the United States, where he would began a long recuperation. He had lost his arm and would be fitted with prostheses. He was on his way home, and he was alive!

John Smith and his cameraman left on their corporate jet back to the United States, and a new film crew arrived on the ground the same day. Smith introduced them to me before he left and told them about Buster. I told them that the Army could use them a lot more than the Marines!

The chief had been put into a figure eight sling due to his collarbone being broken, and I, well, was in the operating room about thirty minutes, getting fragments out of my hip. They retrieved all but four; those were too deep to use a probe, so they left them in. So much for passing through metal detectors in the silent mode! Since then over time, the remaining four fragments have come to the surface and worked their way out, the last one around 1985.

After about ten days, I was back to 80 percent normal and ready to rejoin the team. The doctor told me I could stay in the convalescent ward and stick around for the Bob Hope show, coming the twenty-second, which happened to be Thanksgiving. I told him, thanks but no thanks; I would rather be with my men, and would like to rejoin them as soon as possible. The chief had only recovered about 50 to 60 percent and was still in a figure eight; he too requested to be allowed to go back, but I told the doctor not to let him return until he was out of his sling. He was upset when he found out he wasn't going to go back with me. I needed him in a lot better shape than he was. I told him to give Ann Margret a hug from me and to thank Bob Hope for all he is doing for the troops!

I arrived back at the corral the next day (21st), and all was well. It was good to be back with the guys I loved. They were family; and family is supposed to be together during the holiday season! The word was that the battalion cooks were going to bring out a holiday feast on Thanksgiving Day!

Buster was doing great and was glad to see me, and I him. He was jumping around, barking, and having a great time! I never saw a dog so happy! We all thought Buster was the greatest dog in the sense of Rin-Tin-Tin!

On the afternoon I returned to the corral, "The Cub" (Lt. Daniels) summoned me to the CP. I just knew I was going to get reprimanded or even worse (maybe a courtmartial and probably deserving of one) for the correspondent, John Smith, getting shot! I reported to the lieutenant and the conversation went something like the following: the lieutenant said, "Good to have you back, sergeant. How are you doing?" I said, "Doing fine, Sir. It's good to be back." "I heard about Little, and I'm glad he is going to be all right," said the lieutenant. He went on to say, "It is my duty to inform you (hear it comes, I thought), that you have been recommended by the company commander and me for the Navy Cross." "The Navy Cross! What for," I ask? The lieutenant stated, "What for! For what you did out there on patrol! That's what's for!" I stated, "My entire team that could stand on their feet did the same thing I did! Are you putting them in for a medal too! Because if you aren't, I want that recommendation retracted! I refuse to take full credit for what happened out there, Sir! However, I do take full responsibility for my men getting hit on my watch! That wasn't supposed to happen! Also, there were three men put on that chopper, sir; I only carried one!" The lieutenant stopped me, "Hey sergeant, hold on a minute, you didn't let me finish! Your entire team, including Seaman first class Hopper Cpt. Chu ^ e, and two Navy Seals, have all been recommended; and you, sergeant, also have already been approved for the Purple Heart for wounds received in action!" "Well, what about Buster, sir; he received wounds, too, and he got in the line of fire while we were headed for the chopper, I asked?" The lieutenant said, "As much as I would like to recommend Buster, I don't think it would be very well received by the higher brass!" "Why not try and find out; the worst that would happen is a denial. However, all of us in the team don't feel we did anything of valor. We were just doing our job! We could refuse whatever citation they award us, until they approved Buster! What do you think, sir; you think it could work," I asked? The lieutenant stated, "All of you think a lot of that dog, don't you?" I replied, "Yes, sir! He has saved our butts more times than we can count; and you should think a lot of him too! He saved your ass once!" Lieutenant Daniels responded, "You are the third person to tell me that; I guess it's worth a try." "Thank you, sir," I said. The lieutenant stated, "I just hope I'm not laughed out of the Corps for recommending a mutt for a citation; now, get out of my sight before you ask me to recommend a posthumous Purple Heart to that snake you killed the other day!" "Yes, Sir! Thank you again, sir," and on that I exited.

When I told the guys about Buster being recommended for a citation, they were ecstatic. They all said, if any dog deserves a citation, he does! Hayes ask, "What about the Purple Heart? He deserves the Purple Heart too! He got wounded, didn't he?" I responded, "Chitchester, you go to the lieutenant and ask him about that; I've worn out my welcome!" The Scrounge stated, "Okay, I will! If he kicks me out or refuses, I'll steal his Purple Heart and give it to Buster!" And I believe he would have!

When Lieutenant Daniels presented the forms for citations for my team, he included Buster. The battalion commander stated that Buster was not an official member of the Marine, Canine Corps and was not eligible to receive citations. The lieutenant argued that none of our ARVN troops were either, but they receive citations (and well deserving they were) from our government! After considerable thought, the lieutenant colonel said he agreed with him and would recommend to the investigating team that Buster be awarded the Bronze Star and the Purple Heart.

All military citation recommendations go to Headquarters, Marine Corps, and Department of the Navy in Washington, DC, before they are approved and awarded. If you are put in for a Purple Heart, they are pretty much automatic. Some general signs off on the paperwork and it's done. However, citations of valor are a different story. They have to be investigated by a meritorious service team of the respective branch of the military. The Army, Air Force, Navy, and Marine Corps pretty much go on their recommendation, unless that recommendation is challenged. When it is challenged, the challenger better have a good reason and an outstanding rebuttal or the entire recommendation is denied! The individual or individuals being recommended could really care less about medals, especially when it comes to them. I didn't; I felt I didn't do anything but my duty. I only did what anyone else would have done, and I don't think that's valor! It's just a job. All the members of the team felt the same as me. Now, Buster! Well, that's a different story! He took a hit, so one or all of us would live. That's valor, and in his case, his love for us! He was the only Marine, deserving that day!

About two months later, the word came back about the citations. Sleeper, Little, and I all were awarded the Purple Heart for wounds received in action. Nettleton, Hayes, Hatfield, Hoppy and Sleeper, along with me, were recommended for the Silver Star. Nettleton, Hayes, Hoppy, Sleeper, and Hatfield were downgraded to the Bronze Star. My Silver Star was approved but I refused it. I stated to the board that I did not do anything more than my men did and did not deserve more than them; so I was also downgraded to the Bronze Star, at my own request. Buster received an honorary enlistment and the rank of Corporal, a wounded-in-action Canine certificate, for wounds received in action, and a meritorious service certificate for valor under fire and saving lives! We all celebrated Buster's awards! They were a long time in coming, especially his acceptance in the Marine Corps, even if it was honorary! That we did not ask for, but they gave it to him, and we were proud of the Marine Corps for recognizing him! However, Buster's tenure as an official Marine Canine would be short-lived!

Christmas at the Okay Corral

Christmas time in a combat zone is just like any other time in a combat zone, except that it's Christmas! The work still has to be done; 50 percent watch was routine, but there was scuttlebutt (rumors) of the VC saying that they would be launching an all-out attack on all areas in South Vietnam, and we could not take any chances. The watch was increased to 75 percent. Patrols were increased to three times a day, instead of twice. Sniper positions were increased to 100 percent, instead of 50 percent, all to protect our position.

Of the two to three hours a day (twenty-four hours) that we weren't committed to duties, we were dog-tired and rested as much as we could, and tried to stay dry. We managed to talk to one another about what it was like back home at Christmas time, and what the thoughts of what our respective families were doing getting ready for the big day.

Hoppy said, "Back home, the decorations were all put out to perfection. The tree was trimmed on the twenty-first of the month.

The outside lights were hung all over the house, and his mom would make taffy candy, and they all would take turns pulling it. There taffy candy was a tradition dating back to 1890 in their family. On Christmas Eve, the family would walk around the neighborhood and sing Christmas Carols. On Christmas Day, they would wake up and open their presents; and then everyone would make the trip to his grandpa's house and have Christmas dinner. Then everyone would leave, go down to their local homeless shelter, and take food and gifts to the less fortunate!"

Everyone had their turn in thinking of back home. A tear or two came to the eyes as well as we talked about home, family, and Christmas!

Another Christmas in Vietnam and it was time to get back to business as usual; there was a hornet's nest brewing up north, close to the Laotian border, and another long-range mission was being planned; and the Wolf Pack would be going window-shopping!

After the team and I went over our plan over and over again, making sure everyone knew their job, on the eve of our departure, I told the other members of the team to get some rest for an early call. It is this downtime that can be agonizing, to say the least. I would look over at my friends that would be shoving off with me, and my thoughts would wander and hope I did not lose any more of my brothers. I thought of their dreams and their goals that they wanted to accomplish in life; I thought of back home about my dad, wondering what he was doing and if he was thinking of me, and if he would be proud of me. I thought of my friends; Charlie, Richard, and Jerry, reminiscing of the great times we used to have. I thought of my grandfather, wondering if he knew what I and the rest of us were going through, convincing myself he did. I thought of my mother, not wondering what she was doing, but knowing! I knew she would be on her knees to *God*, praying for my safety, for I knew it was her prayers that had kept me safe! Oh, how I missed and loved them all so very much, and longed for the day when I would be reunited with them all! Tears would come to my eyes while thinking back; then reality would enter my mind once again, and I would pray, "*Lord*, please help us to get through this upcoming mission, help me to make the right decisions in leading my team with aggressiveness and caution and do not allow the training provided to me to be absent from my mind. Allow us to be alert and aware of all things and give us the sixth sense. Allow me to be stern in my orders to my men, but with love in my heart. If we should engage the enemy, spare us; give us the courage to forgive him for his deeds, and forgive us for ours, and give us the strength to disable him with massive force. Protect us by cradling each and every one of us, oh *Lord*, in your mighty hand, and have mercy on us, and return us safely from being in harm's way as we defend our country, our precious Corps, and give the right for everyone to be free; but not my will, but your will be done, I pray in Jesus' name, amen!" Then, I fell off to sleep at around 0100 hours, waking refreshed at 0400 hours!

Operation Wolf Pack III

We left on the morning of December 28 and would be jumping in over close to the Laotian border in the Quang Tri province.

The six of us exited the Huey Gunship via repelling down in a small clearing in the jungle. We had camoed up prior to leaving the gunship and got our bearings once on the ground and then commenced to our destination fifteen clicks north, about four miles from the DMZ and along the Laotian border, where a suspected force of two battalions or possibly more of hardcore NVN regulars were gathering. Our mission was to infiltrate, if possible, and gather as much intel as possible and report back to our BHQ (battalion headquarters). Along the way, we detected no booby traps in the area, unlike the other missions we had been on. We had been in heavy terrain since we disembarked and had only gone 9 km (a little over five miles) in just a little over four hours. We were taking a break, eating chow when we heard voices and took cover! If we were detected, not only would we have a confrontation, but we would also have to abort the mission and hump it out of the area as quickly as possible! There would not be any extraction, because of timeliness; the closest friendly forces was the fourth battalion of the Second Marine Regiment near the city of Quang Tri in Quang Tri province, about fifty miles away! I wasn't in the mood for a double marathon run after a confrontation; I did not want to abort the mission either! When we headed for cover, Nettleton left his metal canteen out and when he moved, he knocked it over, which made a loud noise! Immediately we started receiving fire, and their RadOp (radio operator), grabbed his handset to call his HQ! I shot the RadOp and with effort from the rest of the team, all the other members of the enemy (9) all but one were killed! He turned and ran with their radio and was out of sight before we knew it! Our confrontation was over in less than a minute, and so was our mission! We had to abort, if we stood a chance to survive! We were checking the enemy dead for any documents they might have had on then; anything vital that might salvage some of our operation. As we were checking them over and found some papers, we heard a bugle blowing, and that meant only one thing! They were assembling and coming after us! Chitchester said to the dead, "Sorry to eat, then kill you, but we have to run!" With that statement, we took off to the west toward Quang Tri in double-time fashion!

We had to make it to lighter terrain and risk the chance of being a target, in order to make better time. We had a radio, but it took a hit in the skirmish and did not work! We had to hurry and hurry fast, because we were in deep Kiamichi! I did not want to be a resident of the Hanoi Hilton (POW), nor did I want any of my team there either, not to mention the possibility of being a KIA!

We made it to a main road, leading west (highway number one, I think); it took us around forty-five minutes, and from there we set out in double-time fashion on the road. We ran for a solid three hours, or about 30 km (about eighteen miles)! We slowed down to a normal route step to check my map and compass to get a bearing on where we were. If we were to survive this trip, we were going to have to find water! According to my map, 12 km west, in the direction we were going was the Quang River. There, hopefully, we could find water and cool ourselves off. I did not know how far back the enemy was, but I knew he was back there; just how many there were pursuing us was unknown (I suspected at least a platoon size unit. With that mind-set, that size unit would be more than we could handle, without support. There was no radio to call for help, and if I sent up flares to a passing aircraft overhead, I would give away our position! So we were between a rock and a hard place! Not the best situation in which to find yourself! We had to push on.

We reached the Quang River at about 1600 hours when we cautiously approached its banks, making sure that there were no river patrols around. When Chitchester gave the all-clear sign, we first filled our canteens and put water purification pills in them; you have to wait at least forty-five minutes for the water purification tablets to kill any bacteria the water may have in it before you drink from your canteen. We started soaking in the river after filling our canteens. Man, did it feel good! It felt so good I wanted to lie in that water forever! I knew I couldn't, though; we only had a little over an hour left of daylight and decided to continue the trip or set up a perimeter and spend the night.

We had only been in the water about twenty minutes, and out of habit I grabbed my canteen and began to drink. I had it turned up and had already taken about seven or eight swallows when I remembered about how long before my water had been treated. "Damn!" I said, and continued, "I just drank from my canteen!" Nettleton said, "Maybe it's okay." Hatfield stated, "Yah! Skipper, you've got a cast iron stomach." I replied, "It's not my gut I am concerned about; it's Malaria! Don't!" And I say again, "*Do not* drink from your canteens for another (I looked at my watch) twenty-five minutes!"

We were discussing what we wanted to do: go on about three clicks and spend the night or continue, when we heard a noise that sounded like a motorboat! We took cover and waited; the decision might be made for us, as I thought it may be an enemy patrol boat! When it came closer, we all recognized the motor sound; it was the Navy! I immediately looked for a distress flare and activated it! The boat stopped dead in the water for a minute or two, then approached on the ready while we showed ourselves with hands in the air! A loud voice from a megaphone said, "Show and identify yourself!" I said,

"U. S. Marines, Recon Special Ops Team! Can you take us aboard?" The boat skipper verified who we were and took us aboard. We all heaved a sigh of relief when we boarded that boat!

I told the boat skipper of our mission gone bad, without the details of course, and told him we needed to get radio communications back to our unit, ASAP! He called ahead to his command to get permission to bring us to their CP. They said okay, and away we went at what seemed like warp speed.

It didn't take us long to get to the destination, and when we arrived, I contacted my unit to send a routine extraction (nontactical). I was told that we could not be picked up until the next day and asked the navy commander if he could feed and put us up for the night. He told me he could and not to worry. We were talking to our new buddies with the Navy about our having to abort our mission, because a hardcore patrol had detected us, and when fire silence was broken on either side, I decided to scratch the mission. Their Lt. Jg. (Lieutenant, Junior Grade) from S-3 (Intelligence) stated, "The area where you were was crawling with hardcore NVN Regulars and Chi-Coms (Chinese Communists). We suspect over 3,000 in that area based on reports from our boat patrols that we have had in the last two weeks. It's nothing short of a miracle that you and your men got out of there with your life, especially all in one piece!" I responded, "Lt. Sir, we confiscated some papers off a dead NVN we killed in our exchange of fire. My Corpsman can read this, but we didn't bring him along. Can you read Vietnamese?" The lieutenant took at papers I had and said, "This is the soldier's re-enlistment papers. It gives you and me some vital information: 1. It gives his rank, Cpt. It means that that group was on more than just a patrol, most likely a meeting of some sort. They just don't send company commanders out on routine patrol! 2. It gives his unit and his position in that unit. He was the company commander of the first company, fifth Doc Hoi Rangers! That is the best they have, which means they are probably getting ready to launch a major offensive, and soon! We need to get you on that chopper as soon as it arrives; go straight to your commander and tell him that your after action report must include the S-3 section in order to eliminate time! I need you guys up here in force ASAP; we are sitting ducks here, and my bet is they are going to launch an assault on Quang Tri! We are the only outpost between here and a battalion of Marines at Quang Tri! If that happens, we can't hold them off!" I told the LtJg that I always include my S-3 section in after action reports and I would make it happen. The rest of our conversation was mostly small talk, about home and family, while playing a couple of hands of spades.

Our chopper arrived at about 0900 hours in the morning. We said our goodbyes to our Navy SEAL counterparts and new friends and wished them good luck.

We arrived back at the Okay Corral on New Year's Day, 1966. The colonel and my S-3 section commander were waiting on us, and we immediately went into the Company HQ, where I gave my report and the events that had taken place on the mission, making the decision to abort, and the forced march we made; our pickup by the Navy patrol boat; also my conversation with the LtJg. I handed the S-3 intelligence officer the papers we got off the dead enemy captain. The colonel told the team, good work, and then dismissed us.

On the next morning, January 2, 1966, the 1st Marine Regiment (4,000 troops) moved out for Operations Masher and White Fang. I wasn't feeling very well, so I stayed in the rack and told Nettleton to cover for me. A while later Hoppy came over and asked me if I was all right. I told him, I was just really tired, and needed to get some rest. Hoppy knew that wasn't the way I was (Corpsmen know their people and know when something is wrong), so he stuck a thermometer in my mouth and took my pulse and respirations; he took the thermometer out and I had a temperature of 102 degrees! Hoppy went to the lieutenant and told him I had to go to the hospital because I had malaria! I didn't want to go, but I felt too bad to argue with any one, especially Hoppy! When it came to anything medical, not even General Westmoreland would buck the authority of a Navy Corpsman or Army Medic! So I went for another ride to the Da Nang Naval Hospital, where I was admitted for fever of unknown origin, suspicion of malaria. I said to the Doctor, "Ain't this a Royal Pain in the Butt!"

CHAPTER TEN

Am I Dead Yet?

As I was wheeled to the hospital ward I would be calling home for, I don't know how long, the orderly tried to strike up a conversation with me. I was short with him; oh, I answered his questions, but that's all. I not only felt bad, but was upset that I was going to be away from my team. The chief and Nettles would be in charge, and while I had confidence in both of them, I felt it was my responsibility to see to it that we didn't lose any more people, but wanted to be there if we did. I was also thinking about that water I drank too soon on our mission. It may have been the culprit for this. What a stupid mistake, I thought.

When we arrived at the ward, I apologized to the orderly for being short. He told me he understood. Then I met the nurse on duty and the corpsman that would be taking care of me. The corpsman greeted me, "Blaine is the name, and taking care of you is my game! I am the senior Corpsman and Ward Master. You are Sgt. Reeves; well, Reeves, in here everyone is sick, not just you, but everyone, so we keep the noise to a minimum on this ward, where everyone can get their rest. Some we know what's wrong with them and some we don't! The ones we don't know, like you, we will find out. May take us a while, but we'll find out. If there is anything you need, you just call me, and I will do my best to help in any way I can. If you have a problem with someone else, you will not take care of it, I will with the both of you! Questions?" After he said all that, I figured he was out of breath, and if he wasn't, he should have been! I said, "Thank you for those thoughts, Blaine, and no, I don't have any questions at this time." Blaine said, "Good, I will be back to get your vitals in a minute, and to get a little blood."

Blaine was big and tall, about six feet four, and could probably go bear hunting with a switch, and win! He was passionate about his work and cared deeply about his patients. He was from San Diego, CA, and played baseball for the Padres before he got drafted into the Navy. The Padres were a farm club for the LA Dodgers back then. We hit it off great, and when he had some free time we would be talking baseball together.

For the next two days in the hospital, I did not have any fever at all, but I still felt lousy. Every joint in my body ached and I had no energy whatsoever. I felt like I had to die to feel better. On the third day, my fever came back, and spiked to 103.5. They started sticking my finger every two hours to run malaria smears (before you can be treated for malaria, it has to be confirmed, that's what it is). This went on for the next two days. My fingers were so sore, I refused to let them stick my fingers anymore, so they went after my toes for a while. The fever never let up. One time, on the eighth or ninth day in the hospital, it spiked to 104.6, and they were sure they would find malaria, but it turned out negative again. I was growing weaker every day, and had lost ten pounds since being there. I could not afford to lose much more weight. I was already down to 128 pounds. I weighed 182 pounds when I arrived in the country the previous year, and lost forty pounds due to poor eating habits, little sleep, dysentery a couple of times; in other words, just being plain overworked and worrying about how to keep my men in the team alive! If anyone believes there is glory in combat, think again! A person has to do what sometimes is the impossible during the day, and then come back and stand watch most of the night, in the worst of weather conditions. You stay exhausted all the time, and you have a tendency not to even care whether you live or die; and in your mind, it doesn't matter! However, something inside pushes you on! Your will to live! You tell yourself you are doing a good thing, protecting your country from tyranny, and keeping your family safe back home. Another thing that makes you keep going, something you can reach out and touch is your buddies! You live to protect them; do all you can to see that they get home! As I have said several times, we were a band of brothers!

The morning of the twelfth day, and the eleventh night, Blaine came and took my temperature, like he always does, and then called for the charge nurse. The last thing I can remember is that someone said to someone else, "This man has 105.6 and we have to get his temp down stat!" I can also remember asking whoever was there, "Am I dying?" I heard someone say, as they put me in a stainless steel tub of what felt like ice water on a hot body! "No Sgt., you are not going to die; we're going to see to it that you don't!" After that, I don't remember anything, until two days later, when I woke up in a private cubicle with an IV stuck in my arm, a mosquito net over my bed and sweating profusely, but felt very cold. I hurt all over; every joint in my body hurt and ached to the point I couldn't move without excruciating pain. Blaine was in a chair at the foot of my bed, writing in what looked like my medical chart. When he saw me awake, he stood up and said, "Welcome back to the world, Marine! How are you feeling?" "I must still be alive; no one can hurt like this and be dead," I responded weakly! "How long have I been out?" I ask. "You have been out of your head, two days, three nights," Blaine said. "We almost lost you a couple of nights ago. Your temperature went to over 106, 106.8 to be exact! Anyone else, hell, we would have lost them! You're a fighter!" "What have I got, Blaine? Am I going to be all right? When can I get back to my unit, I asked?" Blaine stated, "You have parasitical malaria, and a very bad case of it. Yea, you're going to be okay, providing you do what the doctor tells you. He will be in to see you in a few minutes to fill you in on what has been going on and what has to be done to get you well, so relax and get some more rest." I asked why I was in a private area; Blaine said it was to protect me from any bacteria floating around in the air; my body was so weak and vulnerable to infection that they moved me into an isolated area.

About thirty minutes later, Doctor Reynolds came in, "Hey, Sgt. Reeves, welcome back to the land of the living! How are we doing today?" I stated, "I feel like I have been put through the ringer, Doctor Reynolds." "I'll bet you do," the doctor said, then continued, "I know you have a lot of questions, so I will try and answer them. You have a very bad case of malaria, sergeant. You are in isolation to help prevent any infection that may be in the air, out on the ward, and you will be here in isolation until you get some of your strength back; maybe a week. The IV is to put fluids back into your body. With all the fever you have had (and you are still not out of danger yet; there may be a couple more fever spikes over the next forty-eight to seventy-two hours, but we'll be on top of it), your body is dehydrated, so we're giving it a drink. The mosquito net is for the possibility of any critters that might be flying around. You will have the IV for a couple more days. I have started you on a drug called quinine; it's what is used to kill the malaria germ and is very effective, but it will take some time. If we are lucky, you will be on quinine for only four to six weeks. This drug will make you sick to your stomach, until your body adapts to it. In the mean time, we will give you a shot to help with the nausea and vomiting, when it occurs. While you are in isolation, there will be someone at your bedside at all times. Do you have any questions?" "No, Sir, I can't think of any right now," I responded. Doctor Reynolds said, "Okay, sergeant, let us know if you need anything, and I will see you later."

That night, not only did my fever run back up to almost 105, but I was so sick to my stomach and vomited up what I had eaten at the evening meal, which was beef broth, the only thing I had eaten in three days. I was miserable and felt so bad! I told Blaine to shoot me and put me out of my misery! Of course, he didn't; he wasn't in the business of taking a life like I was; he was in the business of saving one. He and his relief, Corpsman Fellows, were by my side round the clock during my crises. I could not have asked for better care if I had been at Walter Reed.

On the third day after waking up, I was moved back onto the open bay ward; the IV had come out, and I was feeling pretty good; my fever had gone down to 102. I was still on a liquid diet. It didn't matter, though; anything I would take down would come right back up anyway, because of the quinine. About a week after being back on the ward, the nausea had subsided considerably, and I had this irresistible craving for mustard sardines. I hate sardines! Blaine said that malaria depletes the body of a lot of minerals and nutrients, and sardines have everything in it that the body is wanting. So I ate them and loved them! I could not get enough of them! They were delicious! Doctor Reynolds said if he had a way to build a cannery for sardines, he would be a rich man. There were twenty guys on the ward; fourteen of us had malaria, and we were all eating sardines! I ate anywhere from four to six cans every day! I could not believe I was eating those crazy little fish stuffed in a can. Prior to getting sick, I could not even stand the smell of those things, but there I was eating them and loving them!

After three weeks of being back on the ward, I was getting stronger every day and was feeling much better. I would still spike a temperature about every two to three days, but it was low grade, around 100 to 101.

In the following week, I had no fever at all, and I started to believe I was well and requested to return to my unit. Blaine stated, "Not so fast, hot shot; you still have a long way to go yet!" I rebutted, "What are you talking about? I feel fine!" Blaine again said, "Your blood work is still subpar, and besides, you still have malaria! You have another couple of weeks here before you move to convalescence. The doctor will determine when it is time for you to be discharged. Until then, the door is closed!" I responded, "Well, okay! I can't argue with a closed door!" That is the only time I complained about the care I was getting.

Another week passed and I was still on the ward. The doctor and the charge nurse came in doing rounds at the beginning of my sixth week on the ward. Doctor Reynolds asked, "You ready to get out of here, Sergeant?" "You bet I am, Sir," I said very enthusiastically. The doctor said, "Good, I'm going to move you to a convalescent ward. You will go off all medication. You will be there for ten days. If all goes well, you can return to your unit.""Okay!" I said, "That will be *great*, Sir, and thank you for everything!"

Leaving the ward was bitter sweet; I had made a lot of friends there. Friends, who would forever be in my memory; they were very special, dedicated navy nurses and corpsmen. I went around to all the staff on the ward, thanking them for the great care I had received while I was a patient, and hoping someday I could repay them. They wished me the best, and on that note I exited the ward, shifting to the other side of the hospital, to the convalescent facility.

Is it Time to Leave yet?

The RTD/CVF (Return to Duty, Convalescent Facility) was quite a change from being on a hospital ward. All the patients were there to recuperate and return to duty. Some had minor battle injuries, but most were sick with malaria or something else; when we get here, we can function on our own and pretty much go anywhere we wanted, as long as it wasn't restricted. We ate our meals in a consolidated dining facility; all branches of the military ate there. They served only two meals per day there: morning brunch and afternoon brunch. Morning brunch was served from 0630 to 1100 hours, and afternoon brunch from 1530 to 1900 hours. The food was great and they encouraged us to eat all we could. Most of the guys were underweight after being in the jungle and also with sickness, and held an invitation for us to come back as many times as we wanted; I did at first, for about four or five days, and so did some of the others.

We had reveille at 0600 hours, formation at 0630 hours, and light calisthenics and run from 0630 to 0700 hours. After that we were on our own until 2200 hours, which was bed check. That's the way it was, every day. If your doctor ordered you to undergo ten days' RTD/CVF, if you had no reoccurrences of your problem and no complaints, you were discharged from the hospital, back to your unit.

They had a PX, commissary, movie theater, NCO club, and clothing exchange store. They even had softball games and volleyball and basketball courts. I was like a bird out of a cage for the first several days. It had been so long since I had played ball, I wanted in on the action. It was so much fun, back on the field, even though I was a bit ragged around the edges. That didn't matter; I was really enjoying myself!

In the early evening, I and some of the guys would catch the movie at the theater; it didn't matter what was showing, as long as it was a movie. Then we would go back to the barracks and play spades until it was time for bed check. Then we would awaken to another day, and do it all over again; it was great, but I longed to be back with my team. My emotions were mixed; part of me wanted to stay at the RTD/CVF, but the larger part of me wanted to return to my unit, where my friends were; and after my ten-day tenure at what I called the Safe Haven (RTD/CVF), and a total of fifty-five days of being in the hospital, I grabbed my two rifles, pistol, and the rest of my gear and walked over to the tarmac, after a ride over to the air base, and hitched a ride back to the okay Corral.

CHAPTER ELEVEN

Hey guys, I'm Back

I arrived back at the corral, around 1100 hrs, and reported to the Cub (Lt. Daniels). He welcomed me back and asked me if I was ready to return to my team leader duties. I assured him, I was; and I was looking forward to getting back to work. The Cub then told me that the team was on patrol and should be back any time. He told me to stow away my gear and wait for the men to return, and to be present at the after action briefing. I said, "yes, sir," and left. When I got back to my hooch, the guys must have gotten word that I was returning and had the place fixed up with homemade posters of "Welcome Back, Skipper," which made me feel kinda good, to know they hadn't forgotten me.

The team made it back, about 1200 hrs, and boy was I glad to see them! We all had our greetings and reunion, and I thanked them for the posters, for thinking of me, and that I was sorry I had let them down and would try my best to do a better job in the future. They assured me that I did not let them down, just because I got malaria, and that could have happened to any one of them, and to stop blaming myself.

After we were through with briefing, I asked the chief, "Where is Buster?" You could have heard a pin drop when I asked that question! No one said a word! I looked at Nettleton, "Tom, where's Buster?" After what seemed like a lifetime, the chief spoke, "Buster was killed about two weeks ago, Skipper." I sat down on my cot with my head down, and with tears in my eyes, asked, "How did it happen?" The chief continued, "We were in a fire fight here at the Corral, and Cpt. Chu^e was running WD1 wire to set Claymores off and got hit in the leg and went down. We were pinned down and couldn't get to him, so Buster, on his own, went to help the captain. He tried to pull him into the fighting hole but couldn't. When Buster realized he could not get the captain to safety, he lay on top of him and used himself as a shield to protect him. He was shot several times protecting Cpt. Chu^e and saved his life, but lost his. He never attempted to move off the captain. He was a hero to the end! We buried him just outside the hooch and even the colonel attended and gave Buster a hero's farewell; even played Taps!" The colonel repeated what he had said many times about Buster! "Oh, what's that," I asked. The chief quoted the colonel, "Best Damn Marine I Ever Had!"

I asked how the captain was, and the chief said he was in the hospital and was going to be okay, but probably would not return to duty anytime soon. I told the guys, "Well, if Buster had to get it, I believe that's the way he would have wanted it; protecting the ones he loved. Don't you guys agree?" They all agreed with me!

I told the chief, "Get me up to date on what else has been going on while I was absent." The chief and Nettles proceeded to get me up to date, and while they were talking, I could not get my mind off Buster. That dog saved our butts so many times and was such a great friend. I thought back of the times he had confused and disorganized the VC almost singlehandedly when they had attempted to overrun us; they would not have, but he saved lives that night by speeding up the process. I thought about all the times he had detected VC in the area before we knew they were there; he saved lives then. I thought about how Lt. Daniels came to accept Buster as an equal; he saved lives that time as well. I thought about all the times, we were on patrol when he helped us then; so many times he put himself at risk for us, and so many times he returned unharmed. I thought of the citation certificates he was awarded, and his acceptance as an honorary marine, and how happy we all were, and how lucky we were that he chose us as his friends. Buster taught us that compassion isn't only for humans, and that the relationship between souls that are meant to be together never really comes to an end. Buster came to us when we were new to the area of responsibility, when we were scared out of our wits, and he made it a little easier for us. It was then that my thoughts were interrupted by Nettleton with a loud shout, "*Hey skipper*!" I looked up at Tommy Nettleton with tears in my eyes still, "I'm sorry, what did you say?" Tom said, "We will talk to you later about joint operations Masher and White Fang. Are you all right?" The chief said, "If you want to talk, we are all here for you. We have always shared and comforted each other, so what is it; is it Buster?"

I started talking to all the guys in the team about all the preceding thoughts I had on my mind and then said, "My mother is a good God-fearing woman, and she always taught me to love, honor, obey, worship, and trust in the Lord with all my heart, mind, body, and spirit. She also said, if we do that, He will never leave us. She also stated that when the going gets rough, He will send an Angel to protect us and comfort us in times of danger and need, and sometimes we won't even know He has done it. Buster did both to all of us! Was he one of God's angels? You know, thinking back, that dog just showed up one day out of the clear blue; don't know where he came from, and he came directly to us, this team! We didn't choose him; he chose us! He had skills and courage not even a trained canine possessed! Does that seem a little odd to you guys that a Heinz 57 had all those skills and was devoted to us like nothing I have ever seen! I have been around animals; dogs have been a part of my entire life, and I have never known any animal as intelligent as Buster was! Even when he was dying, he never made an attempt to move off Cpt. Chu^e! Maybe God sent him to help us, and when He believed we could go on without him, it was time for him to move on and help someone else! Buster died that day because his body had served its purpose. His soul had done what it came to do and then was free to leave. I believe that! And I know that when each and every one of us has served our purpose, our souls will be free to leave as well. Maybe we will never know for sure, but I believe he was an angel!"

Nettles looked at me and said, "I have always believed that, but I thought if I said anything, you guys would think I was crazy!" The chief said, "Yea, me too!" The other guys confirmed, and we all agreed to put Buster to rest, and accept the fact that God is really here, even in South Vietnam, watching over all his children! Maybe, just maybe, we will see him again!

Later that day, the chief came to me and told me about Operation Masher and Operation White Fang. It seems that the aborted mission we had had resulted in a success because of the documents we confiscated. The joint missions between the 1st Marine Regiment and components of the Army's 1st Cavalry Division resulted in an overwhelming victory! The Marines and the Army destroyed the base camp the NVA had established! The casualty report read: North Vietnam Army, 2,300 plus dead. U.S. Marines, thirty-one dead; U.S. Army: fifty-five dead. You never want to see lives lost, but we had dealt the enemy a huge blow, a humiliating defeat, and pushed his northern, main force back into North Vietnam! It would be weeks, maybe even months before he could reorganize into a serious threat, or so we thought!

Operation Wolf Pack IV

On March 6, Operation Utah was in full swing and the fighting had been on for three days. We had gotten the upper hand on the VC on the morning of the same day and on March 7, Charlie Company of the 1st Battalion, 2nd Marine Regiment was assigned to mop up the mission. There were still quite a number of pockets of resistance in the operation that had to be defeated.

Charlie Company managed to get themselves bottled up in a fair-sized hamlet that was known to be sympathetic to the VC. Instead of us leaving the operation and returning to the Corral, our entire platoon was assigned to go rescue the grunts of Charlie Company. When we arrived (in about thirty-five minutes), the situation was not good! The only way we could get over to that hamlet was to cross the open terrain, through the rice paddies. The platoon started laying down a base of fire while one team at a time would cross the open fields. As my team was crossing, Hatfield got hit with .50 caliber rounds which cut into him! I went back to get him and cried out, "Oh dear Jesus!" Jimmie was dying, his torso completely separated from his hips and legs! His radio was all shot up too; I motioned for the lieutenant to call in an emergency med evac and get Hoppy! Jimmy Hatfield was still alive, though, and I was trying to comfort him until Hoppy arrived! Rounds were flying and landing all around me, and somewhere in the process another round hit Jimmy and he was gone! Hoppy had finally arrived and I stayed there returning fire to protect him! Others from the Delta team came to lay down a base of fire to secure an LZ (landing zone), to pick up Jimmy, and the wounded of Charlie Company. Once the Delta team arrived, I was ordered to catch up with my team! When I arrived, Hays asked me who got hit. I told him, "Jimmy," and that he was gone. And there was nothing any of us could do for him, and he was in God's hands. With tears in his eyes, Hays said, "His soul did what it came to do, and now is free to leave. Amen." That was the first time any of us had ever seen Chitchester cry, but he did that day. I put my arm on Chitchester's shoulder and said, "I know he was your best friend. He was my friend too! Come on Chit, let's get back in the war."

With our platoon's help of laying down a base of fire and launching a suicidal assault on the VC, Charlie Company worked out of the bottle they were in and helped us finished the assault.

The mission was costly! It cost the life of one of my men! L/Cpl Jimmy Hatfield was the first KIA in the team! We all talked about the possibility of being killed or captured, and how we would handle the situation, but I found out that none of us were doing very well in that department!

Jimmy was barely nineteen years old and one hell of a Marine! When I wrote his parents and his fiancé, I told them that; I told them how dedicated he was and how we were a band of brothers. Losing him was like losing a brother. I also told them of the great times we had together and how tight he and Chit had been. How brave he was (and I just wasn't saying that)! He was a brave man, a good friend, dedicated to the team, one of the best communicators (radio operator) in the battalion, and that I was very sorry at his death and their loss.

Back at the Corral, it was pretty quiet in our hooch, heads hanging low; it hit us all hard, but Hays was a basket case. I wanted to say something to him and the rest of the team, but didn't know how or what to say. He was one of our brothers, and saying the wrong thing or saying the right thing the wrong way would prolong our grief and possibly cause friction among us. When you are in a war zone, you have to be on your toes at all times with no distractions, and nothing can preoccupy your mind; otherwise, you can't do your job effectively, and that leads to mistakes; when mistakes are made, someone can't walk away, and sometime it's permanent!

Lt. Daniels came into our hooch; he sat down with us and was silent for a couple of minutes; he started to talk and said something along these lines, "I was reading about the Revolutionary War last night; and there was a patriot mentioned in my readings about a man named Patrick Henry. Mr. Henry was giving a speech in Virginia to a mostly British body in 1775." The last paragraph of that speech and I quote, "Is life so dear, or peace so sweet, as to be purchased at the price of chains and slavery? Forbid it, Almighty God! I know not course others may take; but as for me, give me liberty, or give me death!" What I am trying to say to you men is that Jimmy was a patriot; he loved this country and was willing to die for it, just like the rest of you are, and all the other men in this platoon. Now Cpl. Hatfield was my man too, and it is never easy losing one of your own, but in combat, it isn't if it happens, but when it happens. We must be prepared for this. All of you know that it can happen to any one of us at any time. Now I want to ask all of you a question; and in asking, I want you to do some soul-searching. "Jimmy Hatfield served his country with distinction and honor and was ready to leave this world doing what he loved. Are you willing to do that for each other as he did for you? Hold your heads up high, Wolf Pack, because Jimmy is watching over you; don't let him down!" When the lieutenant finished, the chief spoke up and said, "I won't!" The rest of us followed suit!

Chitchester reached into his rucksack and pulled out a bottle of bourbon, and said, "Everybody break out your canteen; as we did, he poured a little bourbon in each." We all raised our canteens, and Chitchester said, "To Jimmy Hatfield who is with God now. He is guarding the streets of heaven; guard them well, Jimmy, guard them well!" With that we all said, Amen!

Dealing with Jimmy's death for me was a personal one. I had made a promise to S.Sgt. Dan Whitethat I would bring them all home; no one except he and I knew of that. He was back in the United States, and I would have to let him know; I knew that if the situation were reversed, he would tell me. I had failed to fulfill that promise, and suddenly, I had this overwhelming feeling of anger that surfaced in my mind. Up until now the war was a job, a sense of dedication to duty, and looking out for each other, but as I raised my canteen to honor the toast Chit had made, the war would become personal for me. It was time for some payback!

Operation Wolf Pack V

Operation Texas was the battle for Quangh Ngai. We had it! The VC wanted it, and would do their best to get it! We were determined to do our best to keep it! The operation started on the twentieth day of March, 1966; Bravo Company was the point company. First Platoon (our platoon) was the point platoon, and my team (the Wolf Pack), the point for the entire operation. It was my job along with the rest of the team to engage the enemy and disorganize him, by whatever means necessary, and usually by using sniper fire, M-79 grenade launchers, M-60 machine gun fire, and claymore mines.

It was estimated that over 3,500 NVA were there to attempt to capture Quangh Ngai from the American Marines; just between you and me, they should have brought more men. They should have known better than to face off with 1,600 Marines with so little force! The NVA were way over their heads on this one!

When we reached their base camp where the main body of their force were, the chief and I took up sniper positions in separate areas; the rest of the team lay back from us approximately eighty to hundred meters away; Nettles and Hays set out claymores (six of them) approximately forty yards in front of where their positions would be (I had a full team again due to two replacements). When in position, my radio operator called the battalion to move up; it would take the battalion fifteen minutes to catch up to us. We waited ten minutes and Hays started the surprise attack by firing the M-79, while "The Chief" and I were concentrating on their officers; without leadership, they were just a mob, disorganized, and without direction for quite a while! The M-60s started firing immediately after the M-79 grenade hit the ground! Everyone started running for cover, and as they did, the chief and I were picking them off like flies; it was like shooting chickens in a barnyard! Together, the chief and I, in a time frame of about ten minutes, killed over thirty men, most of them officers. Their entire unit was in a state of chaos! When the battalion was in position, we received the word to pull back, so they could launch the killing blow! The battalion continued the assault on the NVA. A lot of them tried to run, but Delta Platoon, who were on the flank and out away from the hard fighting, caught most of them in crossfire; and well, most of the survivors surrendered! The initial battle lasted less than an hour, and the battalion suffered only three casualties. The NVA suffered over 800 casualties!

There were some small pockets of resistance around that took four days to flush out, and at around midday of the twenty-fifth, Operation Texas was declared secure. The final body count for Operation Texas was: NVA: 1,019 dead, 623 captured! American Marines: ten dead, thirty-nine wounded! Semper Fi!

Back at the Corral, things were changing after Operation Texas. A company of Infantry (grunts) would be moving into the place we had called home for so long, and we were moving up north around the DMZ; it was a place we did not want to be, on a permanent basis, but that's war; you don't want to get too comfortable in any place.

CHAPTER TWELVE

The Vision

At the okay Corral on the evening of March 26, 1966, I could not sleep, so I relieved Nettles about an hour early, around 2300 hours. I had been standing watch for thirty minutes or so, looking through starlight for any possible movement in the distance. It was a quiet night, with nothing going on. I looked at my watch and saw it was 2335 hours. I was just about to turn off the night vision for a while and relax my eyes for a few minutes; as I was making my last scan of the area, something caught my eye! I panned back to the image which was about eighty yards out in front of the parameter. It was definitely a man walking upright (he wasn't trying to conceal himself), like he was on an evening stroll! I looked to the right of the image, then the left just for a second, and when I looked back to focus on the individual again, he was much closer, like right in front of me! All kind of things flashed through my mind in only a split second! How did this person get here so quickly? Why is he alone? How did he get here without anyone else detecting him? I was so scared I didn't know what to do! I laid down the starlight and was reaching for my pistol, and there within five or six feet from me was this old gentleman, looking straight into my eyes, smiling, and waving at me! I was so startled to see this man so close to me, and again I was startled; my heart was in my throat! Then I focused on that smile and that face! It was my grandfather! "Grandpa! Grandpa, what are you doing here?" I exclaimed! I reached out to touch him; and as I did, he moved back from me, waving; as if waving good-bye, with that wonderful smile he always had! Then I saw this narrow, very bright light, and as my grandfather was drawn into it he disappeared! I was so drained with emotion; I just sat down in my fighting hole and cried! I didn't know what to think! I asked myself, "What just happened! Did anyone else see this sight! Am I going crazy with battle fatigue or did I just witness a miracle?" Lt. Daniels broke the trance I had been in, "Sgt. Reeves . . . Sgt. Reeves!" "Oh, it's you, sir," I said. "You okay, Don?" "I need a break, sir. Can you wake the chief to relieve me, and come back and sit with me until he gets here, sir?" "Sure will, Sarge. I'll be back in a minute." As the lieutenant left, I was over the initial shock and was shaking uncontrollably! The lieutenant returned in about five minutes, but to me it seemed like thirty minutes, and he said, "Sergeant, what is wrong, you look like you have just seen a ghost!" "I believe I have, sir." "What the hell are you talking about, Marine? You need to get hold of yourself; now just calm down and tell me about this thing you saw!" About that time, the chief came walking up to relieve me and heard the last of the conversation; "You see a spirit, Skipper?" I told him I had, and he said to me, "Being an American Indian, we believe the Spirits come to us to guide us on the right path, to warn us that there is danger, or to leave us a message. Which is it you received?" As the lieutenant saw that I was calmed down from the chief's presence, he stated he was going to continue his rounds and told us to hold down our conversation to a minimum voice.

I told the chief exactly what happened, down to the light and everything. The chief said, "You have nothing to fear; your vision was real; the spirit was your grandfather telling you he was leaving this world to enter into a much better one and not to worry, and that everything is all right." Hearing that from Amick somehow put me at ease. I left and went back to my hooch to lie down and was thinking of what I had just seen. Then it hit me like a light bulb going off in my head! I remembered the last things my grandfather said to me, and I quote, "You will go back and fight. You will be a brave warrior. You will save lives and be honored. You will be hurt and get sick, but you will be okay. When you come home, I will not be here; I go to live with Grandma." I knew then that I had seen my grandfather for the last time here on this earth, and I cried tears of sorrow. Sorrow for myself; then the tears became tears of joy, knowing that my grandfather was in a much better place than any of us can ever imagine; only reflecting on from what I have been told, then suddenly a still and overwhelming peace embraced me, and I wasn't afraid anymore.

Hell's Corridor

On March 30, 1966, we left the okay Corral en route for Quang Tri Province up along the DMZ (demilitarized zone). We would only be eight kilometers from the DMZ and twelve from Laos. This is where the NVA were infiltrating, and it was our job to stop as many as we could.

For the first ten days, we were busy fortifying our area (establishing a parameter, clearing out a killing zone, digging fighting holes, and building bunkers out of sandbags to protect us from mortar barrages. We also had to run day and night patrols and ambushes along with our fortification duties. It made for eighteen—to twenty-hour days for awhile, and our butts were dragging, to say the least; but we finally got all the extracurricular work done, and for a few days, all we did was go on patrol duties.

After we had gotten established, I asked "The Cub" if he thought the VC knew we were here, as we had not run into any enemy in the fifteen days we had been there. He told me that he didn't know for sure, but that most likely they did know, and to be alert. That evening, at about 2100 hrs, we got hit with a mortar barrage. Five rounds of high explosive; one direct hit on one of our bunkers. Hoppy was leaving in five days to go home, as he was due to rotate back to the United States. He was standing in the doorway of that bunker; he took fragments of that mortar in both of his legs, hip, and chest. He was in pretty bad shape, and his replacement, Petty

Officer, first Class Danny (Danny Boy) Johnson was stabilizing him when we got there. Hoppy was awake and in good spirits, talking and telling us he was stupid for standing in the doorway.

The Med. Evac. chopper would not go airborne on that night, so we had to wait until morning to secure a landing zone for the chopper to pick up Hoppy and get him to Da Nang. In just a few minutes, Danny Boy had stopped the bleeding, treated for shock, and had him stabilized; he gave him morphine for pain, and he was doing okay, and Danny Boy said he was going to be all right.

The next morning, the helicopter arrived and picked up Hoppy, and we all wished him the best and told him to write us when he got the chance. Hoppy was going to trans place back to the United States in five days; we were going to lose him and were all happy that he was going home, but none of us wanted to lose him to a VC mortar! As the chopper was starting to lift off, the last thing he said to us was, "Get one of the bastards for me, guys!"

Danny Boy was now officially our Corpsman for the "Wolf Pack," and based on the ability and his coolness under fire he displayed, we knew we had a good replacement.

It's always bad when you lose one of your brothers, and Hoppy was one. He not only patched us up, treated us for jungle rot, but saved a lot of lives while he was with us, and none of us will ever forget him. He was our friend; and even though it was his job to take care of us, he did a lot more. He cared about us in a way no other professional I have ever known did; and we cared about him. Now there were only four of us left that shipped over together. We were a band of brothers!

About three times a week for the next two weeks, between 2000 and 2200 hours, we would get hit with a mortar barrage; and each time, the VC would concentrate on a particular area inside our parameter, and each time one of our bunkers would take a direct hit! It was like they had eyes inside our compound!

We still had sixteen ARVN troops with us and four of them were replacements, and I suspected one of the new guys. I told the lieutenant of my thoughts, and he already had eyes watching them closely. I also told the lieutenant that the mortar barrages we had taken were done with 60 mm; that meant that to be as accurate as they were, they had to be no further away than six to eight hundred meters. I requested to him that the chief and I take up sniper positions outside the compound, and out about where those mortars might be, until we found them. He agreed to the mission, and the next morning the "Wolf Pack" left with two extra men on patrol. The chief and I would not be coming back with the team. We both were equipped with our sniper rifles, starlight scope, two red and green flares each, our Ghillie suit, stationary straps, prick six radio (walkie talkie), one clicker each (a handheld device, which when pushed, makes a clicking sound .This was used to communicate when talking would be a sure give away of our position), and five days' rations; if it took longer to find those guys, we would live off the land, but we were going to find them and kill them, no matter how long it took; failure was not an option! We were sick and tired of getting mortared!

We took up positions in two trees about thirty-five to forty feet apart, fifteen to twenty feet up, facing a clearing approximately 1,500 meters out from our compound. I found a branch of my tree that was pretty big and sturdy that angled out and down, almost ideal for the area of observation. I got into a comfortable position and strapped myself in to keep from falling out in case I dozed off. The chief did the same. On the first two days and nights, there was no activity at all, except for our own patrols. On the third night, we were looking through the starlight scope and saw activity: three silhouettes on the move in the direction of the base camp 650 meters to our front; one carrying a 60 mm mortar tube, and the other two with rifles and possibly mortar rounds. The chief motioned that he would take the one on the left, and I the one on the right, and both the ones in the middle. They continued to walk toward our base camp; while the chief kept his eyes on them, I took a quick scan to see if there were any more of our little yellow brothers around; I didn't see any, and then turned back my rifle on the mortar group. They were still walking to get into position, and then they stopped and started setting up for their attack! I turned my scope on the chief, and he, me; I held up five fingers. Five seconds to sight in, then count to five, and on five, fire. We got them in our sights in five seconds, and held up one finger, designating the start of our count (we had to fire simultaneously to keep them in position or we would possibly lose the other two), counted; 1, 2, 3, 4, and FIRED! As I fired, I said, that one is for you, Hoppy! All three went down! It looked like one of us got two kills with one shot; I didn't have the angle, so it must have been the chief! We kept our sights on them to make sure they stayed down. *They did*! After two hours of watching to see if our subjects were not playing possum (the VC had great patience), I broke radio silence about 0300 hours and told the lieutenant that we needed a patrol out to confirm kills and to pick us up. On the next morning, we climbed down from our positions we had been in for three days; we had not moved from that place for over seventy-two hours with only repositioning every now and then. All you deer hunters, try sitting in a tree stand for that long; it's a killer!

Before we could climb down, we had to get the circulation and stiffness out of our legs, which took over five minutes; and after landing on the ground, we slumped over for over a hundred yards. I gave the patrol our position and the area where the kills had taken place. They swung by and picked us up first and then went to the killing site. There were three bodies, and the 60 mm mortar tube, along with the ammo on two of the VC. "Mission accomplished, guys, the chief said, and continued, Let's go home!" Semper Fi!

The Visitors

We had been back at the base camp for a couple of days when two old Mountain Yard men and two boys in their teens showed up outside our concertina parameter. G/Sgt. Blankenship, our Platoon sergeant, and Lt. Daniels went to greet them. The Gunny spoke fluent Vietnamese. After they talked for a while, the Mountain Yard people left, and the Gunny and the lieutenant returned. The Gunny came to me and said, "Sgt. Reeves, you and your team get your gear, we're moving out, and bring your Corpsman; I'll brief you later!" When the Gunny tells you to do something, you don't ask questions; you do it!

We met up at the CP bunker and waited for the briefing. The meeting with the Mountain people earlier was about getting medical attention to some of their people who were sick. The Gunny told them to bring their people to us and we would treat them and give them food as well. They refused to do so, because they were afraid the VC would see them. The old man, who was the chief of the village, told the Gunny that the VC had already taken two of their young men, and when they refused to fight for them, had killed them! The Gunny told them that we would go to them; and not only would we give them food and medical care, but we would also provide them with protection, if they would show us where the VC were that were doing this to them. They agreed, and left the two boys behind to show us the way to their village.

When we moved out, the native boys took point and Hays remained behind them as our point. Their village was a little more than two clicks from our base camp and through the jungle. They had their village fairly well protected with the primitive-type mines I have mentioned earlier that the VC used. When we would come to one of them, the boys would point it out to us. The boys had crossbows that they made. The Mountain Yard natives made all their weaponry and were very efficient with them: crossbows, recurred bows, spears, and arrows all to perfection. They lived very much like our Native Americans did many years ago. Here is the good part. *They were on our side*!

When we reached their village, the boys made a type of whistling sound as a warning that they were coming into the village, and another sound from inside indicated, all clear; and the boys continued entering. After entering their area, they welcomed us. The Gunny told us to be on our toes and to split up in twos and mingle with the people; the Gunny and Danny Boy went to where the village chief was and started rendering medical care. While there, they asked us if we wanted anything to eat. We said, "yes"; and the reason we said yes is because, according to their custom, it is considered an insult to refuse food when it's offered. Well, we certainly did not want to insult them; besides that, we were out numbered about fifteen to one! We found out that the meat was monkey, kabob style (on a stick), and it was *good*! At least the way they fixed it; a little course and stringy, but the taste was delicious. We talked with them and made friends and the experience was great.

We stayed with them for about three hours, while Danny Boy treated the sick. Most of the sickness was due to open sores that were infected and causing fever. For some of them, Danny could not do anything because they were so old; but he helped a lot more than not. Before we left, the Gunny told them that he would order food and more medical supplies; and that when they arrived, we would return with them and teach them how to care for themselves.

Our trip to the Mountain Yard village was a very productive one. After returning to case camp, the Gunny reported to Lt. Daniels what we accomplished and in what areas the VC were working; that is where we needed to concentrate our patrol and ambush efforts. For the next two months, we encountered the VC almost every time we went on patrol and/or ambush. We had the upper hand by receiving the information we needed to find them. I started neglecting to say my prayer when we went out, something I never forgot to do since the first day I arrived in the country. I started to feel like I was indestructible, and I could do no wrong. Hunting the VC became a game, and we were beginning to get a little sadistic in our killing of the enemy. I took no prisoners even when they gave up. I didn't want to bother with them. They were easier to deal with dead! When we would shoot them, I would take our K-Bar and carve them up, sometimes beyond recognition, and repeating profanities! I was getting to be an animal on the prowl looking for my prey! I had been in combat for so long (the first time, four months, and this time, over sixteen months, with no word on when we would be leaving) that I thought we all would be there for the rest of our lives. With no end in sight to the war, and back home, all the reports of the demonstrations against the war, and the home folks spitting on the troops and treating them like they were the scum of the earth, I didn't care if we made it back. At least over here, there were people who appreciated what we were doing. The only people I cared about was my team; I didn't care about myself. I was losing my will, self-respect, and my respect for others; some of the guys said, "I had a lot of guts," but that wasn't true. It doesn't take guts to be crazy; and that's what I was: just plain crazy! The horrors of the war were playing tricks on me, and I didn't want to sleep, because I would relive the past experiences all over again in my dreams. The team joined me in getting drunk; drunk out of our minds on the rock gut rum, and tiger rue beer we bought off the locals. We sometime even went out on patrol drunk!

The platoon commander, Lt. Daniels, warned us twice about our excessive drinking, but we ignored him. When he came to us a third time, he put all of us on report. I told the lieutenant, "It's my team, and I am responsible for them," so I am the only one who should go on report. He said, "If that is the way you want it, that's the way it will be, but you will be the fall guy." I told him, "So be it!" On the next day, I went in front of the colonel with an article 32. The colonel asked me if I had anything to say in my defense; I told him a resounding no! My punishment was a demotion in rank down to corporal, thirty days loss of pay, and loss of team leadership. When I left the colonel's office, the Gunny who chased (escorted) me asked me what I got. I told him "Well, I still have two stripes." The outcome was severe, but not as bad as it could have been. I looked at it this way; I lost a stripe, thirty days' loss of pay; I would never miss the pay, because all my pay except ten dollars a month was going home to my bank account. The chief could run the team as well as I could, and I figured, if I could stay out of trouble, do my job well, I would have my stripe back in a year at the most; that is, if I lived that long, and if not, it wouldn't matter anyway! I took the fall, and the team still had their respect with the rest of the platoon.

We stopped our drinking and tried to change our attitude about the killing, but battle fatigue (now called, PTSD) had set in; it was not only me; it was the whole platoon. It hit some of us harder than others. We sure did need some good news!

The Destruction

During the middle of May, 1966, the word came down that the Mountain Yard village and the two squads of infantry assigned to them were being attacked by a company of NVA and were about to be overrun! The entire platoon moved out to the village, but by the time we arrived, they had already been overrun, and the enemy had control of the village! The infantry unit had called in air support, but it did not arrive until after we got there. The gunships were firing rockets into the village, and we were launching M-79 grenades and automatic fire onto the enemy. All our people inside the village and the Mountain Yard people were dead; women, children, all the men . . . everybody; it was a ghastly sight! When the air support lifted, we attacked the Mountain Yard village with a frontal assault and were able to regain control of the village. Almost all of the enemy was killed, and the rest of them ran when they saw they were beaten; the gunships went after the ones who were running.

We called in routine multi-medical evacuations for our dead infantry comrades, and one emergency med evac for two of our men who were wounded in the assault; they weren't from our team. We were searching hooch to hooch for possibly hiding NVA and any more dead. I had just come out of a hooch and was going into another one when Nettleton said, "Hey boss, I'll get this one, you get the next one over!" I said, "No, Tommy, you know how we do this. This one is mine and yours is two down from here!" He said "what difference does it make as long as we check them all?" As he walked through the threshold, there was a huge explosion that blew the entire hooch to rubble, and Tommy along with it! We found out later that the explosion was caused by one of the Gunship's rockets that did not explode on impact. I had lost my best friend, and it was my fault! How will I ever live with myself!

The body collection unit arrived along with the helicopters, and after they done their job, we went back to base camp.

After the death of Tommy Nettleton, I have never been the same; as I said before, he and the chief were my best friends, and I had just lost one of them! As the assistant team leader, I should have ordered him not to go into that hooch; he would still be alive. I would have gladly traded places with him, even knowing now what would have happen. It has been forty-five years, and there hasn't been a single day in all that time that I don't think about him giving his life for me; and I still ask, "why?"

Three days later back at base camp, the lieutenant got the word; in ten days (June 15, 1966), we would be replaced by another Special Operations Recon Unit from the third Marine Division, and would be pulling back to the Da Nang Air Base, for departure back to the United States; we were going home!

The Trip Back Home

Hurry up and Wait

When the word came down about when we would be leaving, it seemed like a huge weight being lifted off me, off all of us. We were so happy to be leaving South Vietnam after nineteen months, all the guys were cheering, and shouting, and broke into chanting. I told the chief to calm them down, and reminded him that we still had ten days here; and that the rest of us needed to leave in one piece.

Funny how good news, or bad news for that matter, can change the attitude and your whole outlook on life; one minute we didn't care whether we lived or died, and the next minute, we were all jumping for joy, telling one another the first thing we were going to do when we got home. We all imagined that the United States was the same, and the situations back home were just like we left them, and we could all just pick back up where we lift off. If only it had been that simple.

We had to run a couple more patrols in the ten days we were at base camp, and then June 15 finally came. We loaded up on the six-bys (deuce and halfs for your Army personnel) and left, heading for Da Nang. We were put in the transient area to get the rest of our personal gear we had to leave there when we first arrived in the country; we were assigned a tent and grabbed a rack (bunk) and started to reflect back on the experience I had gone through the past twenty-nine months, while the others were celebrating the anticipation of going home. I thought about my first casualty, S.Sgt. Dan White, and the promise I had made to him that I would bring the rest of the team home! I broke that promise to him! I wasn't good enough to do it, not like he would have been. All of us had received wounds from the war, some that will never heal! White, Hoppy, and Little got an early ticket home for their physical wounds. Hatfield and Nettleton died on the field of battle. They were only nineteen years old! Hatfield never saw his dream of becoming a stockbroker and making those millions; he always talked about helping others reach their dream, and in time he would reach his. Nettleton was denied his dream of seeing his younger brother play third base at Yankee Stadium. I ask myself, Why; why do the good have to die so young? In answer to that question at that time, I couldn't help but feel in some way that I was at fault because I had broken a promise; and I asked the question, "How will I ever live with myself?" There would only be three of us going home together: Sleeper ("The Chief"), Hays ("Lover Boy"), and me! Why the three of us! Did God have a plan for us triplets or were we just lucky?

The shower felt really great as I stood in total relaxation; it had been almost three months since I had had a shower (since my hospitalization); it was longer for the rest of the guys. We got the word that we would be leaving on the first leg of our trip the next morning via C-130s bound for Okinawa; there we would spend three days and board commercial planes at Kadena Air Force base bound for El Toro Marine Corps Air Station, Santa Ana, California. We stayed at Da Nang for over two months. Time dragged by so slowly that I thought our time to leave would never come; but if a Marine waits long enough, the word comes down on August 22!

When we lifted off at the Da Nang Air Base, we all shouted, "*Good-bye, Vietnam*!"

The C-130s were a bumpy ride, and we were packed in like sardines, but we finally made it to the Rock and were told that we would not be leaving in three days; there were a lot of troops ahead of us, and had three days' manifests to fill. There was also a typhoon coming and going to hit the north part of Okinawa (which is where we were on the island), in four or five days, and all commercial aircraft were ordered to Guam to wait out the storm, the day after tomorrow. So, we were stuck on the Rock for a while and no liberty was authorized because of the typhoon; but we experienced recon Marines knew how to get around that!

Eight of us decided when it was dark that we would sneak out and go into town. We donned dark colors and made our way underneath the fence and through the woods, and humped it to Gotemba (the little town about two miles from the post. The wind was not bad at that time, only about thirty miles per hour. We made it to our favorite bar, the one we used to go to when we were stationed there. We stayed only two hours and started back, because we knew they would be pulling a bed check around 2300 hours. On the way back, we decided to get bold and walk straight through the main gate. Wouldn't you know it, no one said a word! We all walked through that gate like we were supposed to be there! After we were about thirty or forty yards inside the base, the MP came out of his office shouting, "Hey, you guys, get back here!" Well, we took off running into different directions with the same destination in mind, our barracks! Well, he called the Provost Marshall because one of the guys (L/Cpl Berry from another team) that went with us did not make it back. At formation the next morning, the Gunny said, "I want to know who, besides Berry, jumped the fence and went AWOL last night!" No one said a word! The Gunny continued, "I already know who all of you are, so if you don't fess up, it will go real hard for you!" Everyone stayed silent. He went on to tell us that if we confessed, we would only get a reprimand; but if we didn't, we would be facing an article 31. We did not say a word; and we knew Berry would not tell, so the Gunny's bluff was called, because we knew he didn't know who we were, and he was not going to know who we were when we would do the same thing again that evening! We were only planning to go into town just for the one night, but now it became a recon mission that we could have some fun with; so we decided to go into town every night we were there, just to screw with the Gunny's mind.

That evening we decided to wait until after bed check before we decided to go under the fence. Bed check was at around 2200 hours; about thirty minutes after bed check, the chief, Chitchester, I, and Johnson (a guy from Berry's team) took off. The wind from the typhoon had started to pick up to about 60 to 70 miles per hour. We made it out okay, went to the bar, had one beer, and started back. On the way back, we saw an MP vehicle and hid out until it passed; we made our way back to the fence where we went out but saw a sentry and had to divert our mission. We decided to go in through the motor pool. When we were about halfway through, we were detected by another sentry, and we split up again to confuse the sentry but another sentry inside the motor pool compound showed up and that made matters a little harder. Johnson and the chief were caught; Chitchester and I made it back okay. Later that morning, Johnson and the chief showed up. The chief talked the sentries into letting them go. I couldn't believe it!

On the next morning in formation, nothing was said about anything except that the typhoon would hit the island sometime the day after tomorrow. Chitchester and I decided we would go a third time that night. We only decided to sneak off this one last time just to prove that we were better at not getting caught than the Gunny was at catching us. It was one of those things you had to prove to yourself; and besides, we had to pay back the Gunny for all the hard times he had given us during the last three years. However, I would not recommend to anyone that reads this to be out in the elements of a Noah's flood and winds exceeding 100 miles per hour, without any support at all! All the "Lover Boy" and I had to cling onto was each other; and that wasn't much due to the fact that our combined weight was just over 250 pounds.

We made it off the base and our plan was to be gone for an hour and a half; we knew that no one would be open in town, but we went anyway. It was tremendously difficult walking in 110 mile an hour winds; and the rain was so hard, it was like needles sticking in us, but we kept going. It normally took us about twenty to twenty-five minutes to get to town, but this time it took us over forty-five minutes; so when we arrived, we turned around and headed back. Chit made the statement as we were going back, "Hey Skipper, after all we have gone through, it would be a crying shame to get blown away by a damn typhoon, wouldn't it?" "Yep it would, I replied," and continued, "but let's not think about that right now. Let's concentrate on getting back to the barracks!"

We finally made it back to the barracks about 0130 hours; we had left at 2245 hours. We were soaked and wet and chilled to the bone; and we were glad our little excursion was over. Now we could lie in the barracks like the other good little Marines and wait out the storm.

At noon the next day, the storm hit the camp with a vengeance: torrential rain and steady winds exceeding 150 MPH, and gusts up to almost 200 MPH! The media stated that the storm was the worst Okinawa had seen in over fifty years. Usually when a storm of that magnitude arrives on land it starts to lose strength, but this one didn't! The northern part of the island is only 22 miles wide, and the typhoon including the outer band was over 100 miles in diameter. For about fourteen hours the storm hit us with all it had, until she moved on back out to sea; after it left, we helped the permanent party Marines clean up some of the debris. Then we received the word; the commercial jets had lifted off from Guam and were on the way back to "The Rock," and we were to board the buses to Kadena Air Force Base. This time we were really going home!

We waited again for three days for our flight to arrive; it seemed like all we were doing on "The Rock" was to hurry up and wait! Our flight did arrive and we finally boarded the Northwest Airlines, Boeing 707, on September 10; we were scheduled to arrive at El Toro on September 9. Figure that one out! Never mind, I'll tell you! When crossing the International Date Line, heading for the United States, you go back a day, due to the time zones; so we arrive the day before we left! Oh, how sweet it is!

I was finally going home! After twenty-eight months; 244 patrols; 161 ambushes; twenty-eight recon missions, and nine major campaigns, I was finally going home! I was bringing home the hardware as well: Armed forces Expeditionary Medal; National Defense Medal; Vietnam Service Medal; Vietnam Campaign Medal; Presidential Unit Citation; two Purple Hearts; and my country's fourth highest honor, the Bronze Star Medal, with combat Valor. Not bad for a snotty-nosed country boy from Arkansas. What are they worth? I'll tell you what they are worth; I can take every one of them to a bar and trade them all in for a glass of beer if I give the bartender two bucks along with them! What are they worth to me? Memories of a time past; honor of having served with the greatest bunch of guys that ever lived; honor of having served the greatest country on earth, the United States of America; honor of serving the wonderful people of South Vietnam, and their quest for freedom; reflection and the camaraderie of my team and the hell we went through together; the blood spilled in a war no one understood or even wanted to; a reminder to never forget the 58,000 plus deaths and over 350,000 casualties; Tommy Nettleton, Jimmy Hatfield; gone, but not forgotten, etched in my memory forever! Yes, those medals are worth something to me; they are priceless! Some people say, "You are a hero!" No, I'm no hero; just a Marine who tried to do his duty to his country; who tried to protect his friends and brothers in arms, and failed miserably. Tommy Nettleton, Jimmy Hatfield, and the other 58,000 plus men and women who died: I say to everyone who reads these words, "Look up to heaven. Take a good long look, because they are your heroes!"

Our trip back to the United States took ten hours, with stopovers in Guam and Honolulu to take on fuel. We were all quiet and mostly sleeping through most of it; when we did awake, we were asking for something to drink, something to eat or hitting on the beautiful Oriental stewardesses. They would just smile and go on about their business like the professionals they were.

We touched down at El Toro Marine Corps Air Station, 1100 hours, September 9, 1966, and the date hit me; it was my mom and dad's twenty-second wedding anniversary! What a surprise they would have!

I debarked from the plane and touched home soil; I got on my hands and knees, bent down, and kissed the United States soil. I had entered the Marines, gone through grueling training, left my mother three times, left my mother country twice, spent two tours in a war: all of this before my twenty-first birthday. It was so good to be home, and I wanted to celebrate. Little did I know at that moment that there was another war that had been brewing for many months, and it would be much worse than the one I had left. I was in for the hardest battle of my life, the war within myself!

CHAPTER THIRTEEN

I said my goodbyes to my two friends, Sleeper and Hays, while waiting in line to get cleared and told them that I would see them back at Del Mar, after our thirty days' leave was up. The three of us had tears in our eyes when we departed; we had put our trust in each other for so long and now we were going to be separated.

Getting through customs seemed to take a lifetime; one by one was cleared to go through the turnstile, and then it was my turn. They gave my baggage the usual check, according to the regulations back then, asked me the required questions, and gave me permission to go through. I saw my dad, and I was all ready to give him a hug, but he helped me with my duffle and other baggage and said, "Son, I want you to get hold of yourself!" I asked, "Why, what's wrong? Where's Mom?" Dad stated that she was home; they had been coming down there for over two weeks, every day, and she was tired of being disappointed when I wasn't on the plane. I asked again, "Then what's wrong?" Dad stated what I already knew, "Your grandpa Patrick is dead!" I confirmed, "Yes, I know, and I can tell you the exact time he died: March 26, at 11:35 p.m., to be exact!" Dad asked, "How did you know that. We didn't write and tell you, no one did. We asked everyone we knew not to for fear it would upset you too much and hinder you from your duties. How did you know?" I told him about my vision, and he was overwhelmed! Then, with tears in his eyes, he put his hand on my shoulder and said, "It's good to have you back home, son." Without hesitation, I said, "It's good to be home, Dad! I hesitated, then continued, "Hey, it's your and Mom's anniversary.; What have you planned?" "Spending time with you, son—spending time with you," Dad exclaimed!"

Dad wanted to surprise Mom when we got home, so I went along with the gag by letting Dad explain to Mom that I wasn't on the plane again and would have to wait another day. Then Mom would get mad and speak obscenities about the Marines and I was to walk through the door. The reaction Mom had was what Dad predicted; then I walked in. "Hey Mom, I'm hungry! What's for supper?" She turned, looked, and for a moment could not believe her eyes; then tears came into her eyes, and she came running to me, shouting, "My son is home—My son is home, thank you God, my son is home!" I shall never forget her reaction, nor her words at that short reunion we had way back then; oh, what I wouldn't give right now just to see her smiling face for only one second, again—just one second!

The First Chevrolet Camaro Ever Bought

Three days into my leave, I decided I would buy a car with all the money I had sent back to the Bank of America, so the three of us went down to the local Chevrolet dealership and looked around. In those days, the new models came out in September, for the next year. When a new addition to the line of vehicles came out, they chose only one dealership to display it on a certain day. The new addition to the line being presented for 1967 was the Chevy Camaro; and back then, there was an unveiling (had a car cover over the auto) at a precise time and only one dealership would do the unveiling at that precise time. The following day, all the dealerships in the nation could start selling the vehicle, but the dealership picked to do the unveiling could sell the car immediately at the unveiling. San Clemente, Chevrolet, Pontiac, GMC had the unveiling on the 1967 Camaro precisely at 7:00 p.m., September 12, 1966, and we were there. When they took the cover off that car, I immediately fell in love with it; and I bought it, on the spot! It was something, all right; 327 cubic inch engine, aluminum four barrel (AFB), four in the floor, fire engine Red! Just what I wanted! What a car; and according to the dealership, I bought the first one ever sold in the United States!

I was the envy of the town for a while; as a matter of fact, the envy up and down the coast! I drove all over Southern California showing off my little red Camaro. All the girls would flock over to me wanting to ride in my new car; of course, I accommodated every one of them. Most of them showed their appreciation in special ways, and others gave me their phone numbers and told me to call them; and I did—all of 'em! Well, most of 'em? Okay, a few of 'em! Point is, I never had any trouble getting dates back then, and I owe it all to my little red 327 Camaro convertible!

The Decision

Time flies when you are having fun (I mean that literally), and it was time to report back to Camp. My thirty days' leave was up and it was time to get back to work. I had been assigned to the training command at Camp Del Mar to help train the Recon Marines and Navy Seals and get them ready for combat; and in between the career advisor was after me to ship over (re-enlist) for another tour of duty. I was leaning very hard on staying in the Marines. I was getting this argument from my parents, not to. I only had six months left on my initial enlistment, and I had to make a decision fairly quick, if I were to receive shipping over bonuses. The bonuses to stay in were very good then. Military salaries back then were not nearly as good as they are now; as a corporal, my annual pay was only $3,600 a year, and the bonuses offered for signing were cash up front of over $10,000; but that wasn't the only reason for my considering staying in. I loved the Marines; I knew it was what I wanted to do with my life, but my parents were bearing down hard on me! I did not want to disappoint my mother, but my mother could not live my life either; that was up to me. When it came right down to where the rubber meets the road, so to speak, the decision was up to me and only me; and I would have to live with that decision, right or wrong! If it turned out to be the right decision to leave the Corps, then no harm, no foul; if my decision was wrong to leave the active duty branch, I had two years of reserve duty and during that time, I could request active duty without dropping a pay grade. That $10,000 bonus sure would be nice, though!

I met with the career advisor on March 15, 1967. He offered me my Sergeant, E-5 rank back, my choice of duty stations for one year, and a $12,500 cash bonus, spread out over a six-month period, with $6,500 of the money up front, at the signing! My first response was yes; then he put the papers in front of me to sign. I looked at them, picked up the pen and looked at him, and asked the question, "What is the chance of my returning to Vietnam?" He responded, "With the critical MOS (military occupational specialty) you have, it is highly probable you will be back there within a year." I looked down at the papers for a few seconds, then pushed them back to my career advisor, returned the pen back to the table where it had been, and told him, "I have to decline the offer." My reason for declining was simple; I knew within my gut that I would not survive another tour in combat at that time in my history. I left the rank, the money, and the choice of duty station on the table and walked away. My active duty was up on March 28, 1967, and from the fifteenth all the way to the twenty-eighth, I wrestled with my decision, but the combat factor kept popping up; and on the twenty-eighth of March, 1967, I left my beloved Marine Corps!

CHAPTER FOURTEEN

Back to Civilian Life

I left California and decided to give the great State of Texas a try. I had heard that the city of Houston was in need of police officers, so I thought I would apply. I had traded my Camaro in on a Plymouth Barracuda, so I loaded up the Barracuda formula "S" (Kingfisher) and hit the road. I took my time getting there, stopping along the way seeing the sights. I had forgotten how beautiful this country was, and I was enjoying every square inch of it!

When I rolled into Houston, I was blown away by the size of this city; it was spread out all over the place. I stopped and got a room and unloaded my car, then went to the motel clerk and asked him for a map of the city, and inquired where the main police precinct was? He didn't know, so I guess I was on my own. The next morning, I hopped in my car and decided to do a little intelligence work; in other words, I stopped a cop and asked him where the police station was? He gave me directions, and after the routine wrong turns and being on the wrong freeway, I finally made it downtown to the station. I told the desk sergeant what I was there for, and he asked me if I had taken the civil service test, and I told him, "No, I had not." He informed me that the test had to be taken and passed before I could apply. He gave me the dates and place of the test schedules and said I had to apply to take the test. Well, I just didn't want to go through all that red tape; I didn't have to go through that mess to enlist in the Marines; why would I want to do it now? I got back into my car and started driving around, wondering what happens next! I must have driven for over an hour, and out of the corner of my eye, I couldn't believe my eyes! A man came up from behind a woman and snatched her purse, knocking her down in the process, and took off running; all the people who witnessed the thief went on like nothing happened! No one even offered to help the poor lady up! I turned the corner in the direction of the thief, and when I found a place to pull over, got out of my vehicle and pursued the thief on foot, thinking: "Where is a cop when you need him?" When he saw I was about to catch up with him, he threw the purse down on the ground and continued running away! I didn't run after him after that, because I had accomplished my mission: getting the lady's purse back! I walked back to where the lady was, and by that time, several concerned individuals were gathered around consoling her. I made my way through and asked her if she was all right and returned her purse to her. I asked if she needed a ride anywhere; she said no, but she could use a drink, and asked if I would join her? Well, of course I said yes; after all, she was a victim, she was attractive, and at that moment, I was her hero; wouldn't you? Besides, I felt she needed some *special consoling*! So we went to a club across the street and had a drink!

It turned out through the course of the conversation that my very attractive victim was very married! That special consoling would have to be left to her husband! A couple of good things did come out of that experience; I met two very special people, who became my friends. Jim and Sue opened their home and their heart to me; they were one of the few people who didn't look down on Vietnam veterans. I told them that I was only passing through and had not decided where to stay in Houston, but they insisted on my staying with them for a few days anyway, at least until I could get settled or decided what to do. I agreed to the loan of their spare bedroom, only if I paid for the room. Jim and Sue were very much in love with each other; and I thought, if I was ever lucky enough to get married, that's how I wanted it to be.

Jim was a karate instructor for the IKF (International Karate Fraternity) chapter in Houston. He got me an interview with the Headmaster, where I took a practical application test, and was hired to teach their basic self defense class. It didn't pay much, only $ 65 for a twenty-hour work week. The hourly pay was excellent, twice as much as the national minimum wage was back then, but I wasn't happy. I just didn't like Houston, TX, and I was restless. I stayed there and worked for about three months, saving as much money as I could, then said my goodbyes to Jim and Sue, and thanked them for their wonderful hospitality. Then I pointed the Kingfisher east and hit the road, stopping at several places: New Orleans, LA; Mobile, AL; Pensacola, FL. Then I decided to run on down to Clearwater since I was in Florida and see if I could find Tommy Nettleton's parents. I wanted to offer my condolences and answer any questions they might have about their son. The thought came to me to do the same for Jimmy Hatfield's parents as well; so that's what I decided to do!

The Meetings of Emotions

When Tommy was killed, I went through his personal effects and found a couple of letters to his parents that he had not mailed. I still had those letters, so it seemed like a good time to deliver them. When I left California, around four months earlier, this was my intention; I thought at that time, it was the reason I was so restless back in Houston, and maybe this would settle me down.

I arrived in Clearwater on a Friday afternoon, stopped at the post office, and asked for directions to the Nettleton home. I thought about calling them beforehand, but was afraid they would not want me to come, so I decided to go to their home unannounced. I knocked on the door and a man opened it. I was so nervous I was shaking, and with a trembling voice said, "Mr. Nettleton, I am Don Reeves; I served with Tommy overseas." Mr. Nettleton invited me in with enthusiasm and introduced me to his wife. They asked me to sit down, which I did, while Ms. Nettleton fixed something to drink. Mr. Nettleton and I engaged in small talk until Ms. Nettleton reentered the room with a pitcher of tea and glasses. She filled the tumblers with tea and offered them to us and sat down. Ms. Nettleton asked, "Are you still in the Marines, sergeant?" I did not mention that I had been busted down to corporal, "I am not on active duty, but still in the reserves." Mr. Nettleton said, "Tom stated in his letters that you were the leader of his team." "I was. We were best friends, and that is why I am here; I have never been the same since his death. I don't know how much you have been told on how Tommy died, but I am here to tell you the rest of the story of what happened that day, if you want, and to deliver the rest of his personal effects to you." Ms. Nettleton asked what they were; and I handed her the two letters, Tommy wasn't able to mail. I stated, "I wanted to deliver them in person." She took the letters from my hand and started to cry. Mr. Nettleton consoled her, and as he was doing so, I continued, "Maybe I should go; I can see by my presence, I have brought back some painful memories for the two of you, and I'm truly sorry!" Ms. Nettleton responded, "No, don't go, please stay awhile longer; we want to hear from you what happened to our son." I sat back down and took another drink of my tea.

I told the Nettletons exactly what had happened, right down to the exchange of words Tommy and I had during the heat of the battle on that fatal day of his life. I told them exactly how I felt then and still do to this day; it was my fault that he was killed! "If I had ordered him not to go through that opening, he would not have done it, because he was a good Marine and always obeyed orders! It was my time to die but he took my place! We loved each other like brothers; him, the chief, and me! I loved all the guys in my team, but the three of us had this special bond. That is what Tommy did that day. He gave his life, so the rest of us might live. I believe it with all my heart." Then I added, "Greater love has no man than that he gives his life for his friends." Before I was through telling what happened, the three of us were in tears. I was crying uncontrollably, reliving that day all over again. Mr. and Ms. Nettleton consoled me and assured me that they didn't want their son to die and told me that I shouldn't feel at fault. They also stated, "Tommy died doing what he loved to do, and that was serving his country as a United States Marine, and we are very proud of him. We are even more proud now that we have heard the whole story. We thank you very much for coming so far to visit with us." "It was a debt I had to pay. The Marine Corps motto is 'Semper Fidelis.' Its Latin meaning is 'Always Faithful.' Believe me, folks, this is something I had to do!"

The Nettletons invited me to stay for dinner, which I did. We made small talk, and they also told me about when Tommy was a child, when even at six years of age he talked about being a Marine.

In total, I spent over four hours with the Nettletons. They were such nice people. I never saw or heard from them after that; but I felt I had done my duty to my friend, and I left feeling good about myself!

My next mission was in Jackson, Tennessee, and it would be a long drive; the "Kingfisher" and I were just plain tuckered out in Tallahassee, so I stopped at a motel and rested for a couple of days. I called Mom and Dad to let them know where I was and not to worry; I was taking care of personal commitments and was working my way home. They didn't understand of course, but I told them, "It is not for you to understand what I have to do; it is only for me to understand what I have to do!"

The "Kingfisher" and I hit the road on a Monday morning, taking our time. I arrived in Atlanta on the afternoon of the same day, and heard on one of the local radio stations that the Braves were in town, and playing the Cardinals that evening; so I decided to follow the signs to the stadium and take in the game. I had never seen either team play in person; and since I had grown up listening to the Cards on the radio, this would be a real treat.

It cost four dollars for a major league game and even back in those days was a real bargain, considering that to attend an NFL game, the price was fifteen dollars. I bought my ticket, made my way through the turnstiles and concessions where I purchased a couple of dogs and a beer (you don't go to a baseball game and not buy at least one hot dog); there is something about the taste of a hot dog at the ballpark! I made my way down on the first base side of the stadium, hoping to find a good seat in the grandstand section, which I did, right between two very attractive young ladies. I asked if the seat was taken, and they invited me to sit down. I struck up a conversation with them, and the three of us hit it off well; so I asked them to show me around Atlanta, and they accepted the challenge. They asked me where I was staying, and I told them I had not gotten a room yet; so they talked it over among themselves and decided it was much more convenient if I stayed with them for a couple of days. Well, I wasn't going to turn down the opportunity of a guided tour of Atlanta, Georgia; besides, from my point of view, Atlanta was starting to look real good!

We didn't stay for the entire game; the Cardinals were beating up on the Braves pretty bad, and the girls didn't like that. I was to follow them to their apartment, park my car, and get into their car where they were going to take me to a place called Atlanta Underground. It turns out that this place was the only part of Atlanta that did not burn when the Union soldiers marched to the city during the Civil War. The Underground was about a block and a half long, and one night club after another. It really is underground! When the city was rebuilt, they built over that area, making it underground; that is why it is called "The Underground." We went to several clubs there; one in particular (I can't remember any of the names), The Platters (a well-known group back then), were playing on stage, and at another place, a country artist by the name of Don Gibson was playing. Both were great, and I was having a great time! Too good in fact; I was about three sheets in the wind (drunk), and got into a fight with some local guys when they tried to put the hit on my ladies, and the security kicked us out of the underground. The girls took me to their apartment where I passed out on the couch and awakened on the living room floor to the smell of bacon and eggs and Lacy laying crossways on my chest. Suzie was cooking breakfast; I got up to see if there was any coffee, which there was, and poured myself a cup. I looked at Suzie and asked, "What happened when we got here last night?" "You made it to the couch and passed out; later on you were talking in your sleep and yelling, don't go in there! Don't go in there! Lacy went in to where you were, which was on the floor, and woke you up; you acted as if you were really scared, so she stayed in there with you." I apologized for my interruption of their sleep and told her, "I have these dreams, bad dreams of the war. I haven't quite adjusted to being back home. I really should go; I have imposed on you nice ladies long enough." I laid my cup down on the counter and started to walk out of the kitchen when Lacy met me, and put her hand on my shoulder and said, "I see you are feeling better this morning. What's this about your leaving? You can't leave yet. In the first place, you haven't had breakfast, and in the second place, we are taking you to six flags today! You can't leave. We don't want you to leave!" "I really should go; I have to be in Jackson, Tennessee, to take care of business." Before I could finish, Suzie said, "Oh god, you're married!" I responded, "God forbid, no. I don't have a girlfriend either, and no, I'm not gay!" "What is so important about your being in Tennessee so quickly then?" Lacy asked. I inquired, "You guys really want me to stay for a while?" Then Lacy said, "Of course, we do. Why do you think we are standing here half naked making fools of ourselves asking you?" Then she put her arms around me and planted a kiss on me that would make a Sailor blush! I responded back with a kiss of my own, "Well, since you put it that way, I guess I can hang around for another day or two! Can we eat now? I'm starving?"

Over breakfast, I found out that Lacy and Suzie were in college, studying social work, and were going to start their senior year in the fall semester; after they received their bachelor's degree, they planned to attain parttime positions in the field and continue on in graduate school working on their master's degree. They had been best friends since sixth grade and pretty much did everything together, and shared their boyfriends while growing up; they still did! The three of us had a great time together during that week, and I must say quite an experience, along with an education, behind closed doors!

They both treated me like I was the most important person in their lives the time I was there; why I don't know! I only know that I grew very fond of them and felt reluctant to leave, but they had their commitments with their schooling and I had my commitment in Jackson, Tennessee.

I never saw or heard from Lacy or Suzie again, but often thought of them in my early years wondering if they reached their goal in their chosen profession; I wonder if they got married and had families; I wonder if they were still best friends. Whatever their destinies were, I hope they received everything good that life had to offer!

I left Atlanta early Sunday morning and arrived in Jackson Sunday evening. I got a room at one of the local motels and lay on the bed unwinding from my trip. I looked in the phone book for Jimmy Hatfield Sr., listed, and wrote down the number for later reference. I then went to the motel lounge and started drinking. The nightmares were starting to get more frequent, and the alcohol seemed to help me sleep at night. I was always scared to go to sleep for fear of having a bad dream, so I would drink myself into a drunken stupor and pass out!

On Monday afternoon, I called Mr. Hatfield, but no one answered the phone the three times I called. On the following morning, I attempted another call, which was unsuccessful as well. I opened the phone book to get the address and decided to drive over to the place. When I arrived, I knocked on the door, but no one responded. I looked in the mailbox for any mail; I wanted to make sure the Hatfields had not moved. There were a couple of pieces in the box, enough to tell me that they still lived there.

I went next door to see if the neighbor knew of their whereabouts; it took knocking on three of four doors before someone opened the door. I introduced myself and asked the lady of the house if she knew how I could get in touch with my subjects? She asked me if I was a friend or relative; I told her no. I told her, "I was in Vietnam with their son, Jimmy, and I wanted to visit with them on his behalf." She stated, "Jim and his wife were in a very bad car wreck; June was killed, and Jim is hanging on by a thread; he is at the, University of Tennessee hospital in Memphis." I thanked her for giving me the information and left the area, continuing west on I-40 toward Little Rock. I wrestled with the notion of stopping in Memphis at the hospital; maybe there would be a relative there I could talk to. I decided not to stop; the relatives had enough on their mind. If I went there, I would just open up old wounds. So when I got to Memphis, I kept on going, and crossed the river in Arkansas, a place I hadn't seen in almost three years. I was so glad to get back to Arkansas that I started singing that song Lefty Frazell recorded several years back:

I hear Little Rock calling,

Homesick tears are falling,

I've been away from Little Rock way too long;

Gonna have a worried mind,

'til I cross that Arkansas line,

I've been away from Little Rock way too long.

I must have sung that song thirty miles. I drove straight to Little Rock, and then on to Bryant, to Mom and Dad's place. Mom was there but Dad was working; I gave her a hug, and kissed her on the cheek, then stowed my gear and belongings in the room she had ready for me.

My Downfall; the Beginning

I hung around the house for the next week or two, trying to decide what to do for the rest of my life. I would read the want ads in the paper to see what jobs were available; nothing caught my eye. About the only thing I was qualified for was picking off a person with a rifle at a thousand yards or sneaking up behind someone and making them a statistic. Back in Houston, I thought I wanted to try being a cop, but I threw idea out of the window; and the little time I was a karate instructor there, it was so boring to me that I wasn't interested in it. I wasn't interested in much of anything, anymore.

I felt lost and lonely in a world surrounded by people, who I felt didn't care or understand me anymore; and I don't think I understood them or cared for them either! The nightmares were getting worse, and I would wake up expecting to be back in the war, only waking up to white pillows and the carpet on the floor! I had to have a drink! I drove three miles to the County Line, to a bar and ordered a drink. The bartender said to drink up quickly because it was closing time pretty soon. I overheard a couple of guys talking about going to an all night club when they left there. I inquired as to where this place was; they told me, and added, "It can be a pretty rough place; sure you're up to it?" I said, "Yes, that's okay, I'm used to rough places!"

That's the way it was for the next eight or ten months; during the day around my friends and relatives (including my parents), I pretended everything was just great, and then at night, depression would set in, and the past would haunt me and I would be in the clubs until the wee hours of the morning. I would come home more often than not with skinned knuckles, sometimes a busted head or a fat lip, and most of the time not remembering anything the next day! I had been banned from so many bars and clubs I was running out of places to go!

I was also running out of money, and my dad was running out of patience with me. He told me to either get a job and settle down or get out! Mom told me that I needed God back in my life. I didn't want to hear about the God thing. I felt God had abandoned me a long time ago and wanted nothing to do with me; I might add that the feeling was mutual! Besides, He didn't want to have anything to do with a person that had made his living killing other people! So, Dad's statement made more sense, so I started to look for work. The real reason was that I didn't have the money to rent a place of my own, so the work thing was a priority!

I bought a Sunday Arkansas Democrat and scanned over the classifieds, circling a few places that I thought would interest me, and set out the following Monday morning. Most places told me to fill out an application and leave it with them, and they would get back to me; then later that day, I met Bill Willkie, the Manager of a local grocery store chain. He took to me right away and hired me on the spot as a Produce Manager trainee. Robert (Bob) Collins was the Produce Manager, and a former Navy cook, so we had a lot in common. He was a little older than me, so his tour of duty did not involve combat; but that didn't mean he wasn't knowledgeable of his old trade. He had an arsenal of funny stories, and he kept me in stitches most of the time.

I would work from 7:00 a.m. to 4 p.m., then go around the corner and drink beer with Bill and Bob until around eight, and then go home. Then it got to be a little longer for me as time went on, until my drinking would last most of the time, after midnight; then I met Sherry!

My First Born

It was a Saturday night; she was sitting at a table with an acquaintance by the name of Jack Walden. She and Jack would get up and dance nearly every dance, but she kept looking at me. A few minutes later, Jack motioned for me to come over; reluctantly I did, because Jack and I had had a couple of confrontations with each other, and I didn't want another. As I sat down, Jack introduced us to one another and asked me if I would dance with Sherry while he took care of what he called "Pressing business."

We made small talk and danced to most of the country and western songs the band played, all the slow ones. After a couple of hours, Jack had not returned, and Sherry said she had to go home, and asked me if I would take her home. I was up to the idea, so I did. Five weeks later we were married and had moved to California; and on January 23, 1969, Don Jr. was born! He was quite a sight! He was my little man! During the delivery, Sherry was cursing me with every contraction, but after DJ was born, we were both bursting with pride! Especially me! A year earlier, marriage and family was not even on my long-range things-to-do list, but here I was, married, and holding my son in my arms. I was overwhelmed with emotion.

When we moved to California, I took a position at a car dealership in Santa Ana where I first broke into the sales field. It wasn't long before I was selling cars at a steady rate and making fairly decent wages, but things weren't going well on the home front. Selling requires long hours and she did not like me leaving at eight in the morning and getting home at ten at night. It resulted in arguments and fights most of the time. It started to affect my sales numbers and my paycheck. I was accused of cheating and all sorts of things. So I left the job I liked and went to work for Safeway Stores, a national grocery chain. After I was there three months, I was asked if I wanted to move to Dallas, TX, and be a grocery department manager, with more pay of course; so we packed up and moved to Dallas. Sherry was kicking and screaming all the way there; I finally told her to shut her mouth and tend to the baby, like a wife is suppose to do!

I didn't like Dallas, Texas, any more than I liked Houston; and after about three months, I was talking to the Retail Clerks Union in Little Rock about arranging a transfer back to my old job at Weingarten's, with Bill Willkie and the gang. Thirty days later, Bill had done some shifting around at the store and made a place for me; so back to Arkansas we went. While in Dallas, the nightmares had started to come back, and the more dissatisfied Sherry grew, the more I drank. I felt I was becoming an alcoholic. It became necessary in my daily routine; without it, I could not make it through the day! With the exception of Charlie (he was always trying to talk some sense into me), all my friends and almost all of my relatives shunned me and would have nothing to do with me! What a way to live, huh!

The nightmares were continuing, and I would wake up in a cold sweat, trembling! Because of the bad dreams, Sherry would tell me that I was weak and could not face reality; that I was inadequate and a poor excuse for a man. At other times, she would tell me that everything was okay and that she didn't mean to say those things to me.

I suppose if you hear something long enough, especially from someone that is supposed to love you, you begin to believe it to be so; at least, that's what happened to me! I was at the point where I did not know what reality was anymore. I would hide everything from my parents. I would usually, in most cases, support Sherry, putting the blame on me! I didn't think Mom and Dad knew we would argue and fight the way we did; of course, later in life, Mom told me they knew. The only person I could talk to was my best friend, Charlie; no matter what time of day or night it was, he was always there for me. He would really listen and always encourage me, offering assurance that there were better days down the road. He was the one true friend I had left in the world!

Mark Anthony

On March 20, 1971, Mark was born, and we were again proud parents; well, at least I was. Sherry had her hopes for a little girl so bad that she went into post partum depression, in the worst way. She had to stay in the hospital an extra four days to get over most of it. When we finally went home, everyone came over to see the baby. Oh, he was a real cutie, and I had big plans for him and DJ. We would go fishing, play baseball, hiking, and all the great things fathers and sons do. A month later, things changed; something wasn't right!

We were at Mom and Dad's, and I was feeding Mark, and all of a sudden he stiffened up, threw his head back, rolled his little eyes back, and started jerking uncontrollably! He was having a seizure of some sort. I thought he was dying! We immediately rushed him to the hospital, where he was admitted! The doctor and nurses worked on him for over an hour before the seizures were under control; fifteen minutes later, he started having them again. A pediatric psychiatrist was brought in on a consult and told us, after several weeks of working with Mark, that he was blind and deaf, along with the seizures.

He finally came to the conclusion that another specialist should be called in, one of the best in the field of Pediatrics. He gave us a very grim picture, one that devastated both of us. Mark had a very acute form of cerebral palsy and would not get any better. He only gave Mark four to six years of life!

Mark was on a lot of medication; almost all of it was anti-seizure drugs. When the seizures would return, the doctor would increase the dosages and add another drug on top of the ones he was getting; he said there was nothing else they could do!

Mark was a very special little boy; even though he could not see or hear, he always knew we were around. His little eyes would light up and there was excitement in his voice, and he had that very special smile on his face that would make our day complete.

CHAPTER FIFTEEN

Army National Guard

I needed to make more money; even though I had insurance, the medical bills were piling up. When I asked Bill at work if I could have some overtime, he told me the District Manager had to cut all overtime out due to profit margins.

Charlie had been after me about going into the Army National Guard ever since I had been home from the Marines, so I decided to give him a call. Three days later (August 1971), I was in the Army, and another chapter of my life was born.

They had a program for prior service personnel, called the "Try One"; you could enlist for one year to see if you liked it, and that is what I did. I tried it, and I liked it.

Charlie was a circuit controller in the Benton, Arkansas unit. It was said that it was the best communications company in the National Guard, and better than some regular Army Signal Corps units. It would be completely different than what I did in the Marines; and I knew nothing about communications, except my cross training on a small radio you carry on your back. These radios were so big that they had to be carried on the back of a truck, and there were over eight of them! It would be a challenge, to say the least.

Charlie immediately assigned me to the operations section, of which he was the NCOIC (noncommissioned officer in charge). He trained me on the circuit control panel, and later I went to school at Fort Gordon, GA, in order to receive the MOS assignment. I had a heads up on everyone else, because I had been operating the circuit control panel for three months. It was a self-paced course, and I completed the four month school in three weeks. I was pretty proud of myself having completed the course in a short time.

When I arrived home, my world came crashing down on me; my wife and kids were gone! Sherry called her parents and moved all her belongings to Indiana.

She left me a note that said something to the effect that I have left with the kids and gone home to Indiana to live with Mom and Dad. Don't call because I won't talk to you. I am getting a divorce! I never wanted to marry you anyway, but I was pregnant with your child and wanted it to have a name. I am going to move on with my life with someone else, and I suggest you do the same, if you can find an idiot like yourself! Good-bye, Sherry.

I was devastated; at first I was hurt, then I was mad, then I thought of my kids. The thought of going through life without ever seeing them again was just too much to take. I thought about ending my life right there; it was already in a shambles! Then I thought, no, if the VC couldn't do it, I'm not going to either!

I went to Mom and Dad and told them what happened, and they too were in a bad state as well. Dad of course told me it was all my fault! Mom reminded him that it takes two people to make a marriage work. Mom and Dad loved those kids as much as I did, and there was no way we of us were going to go down without a fight! A week later I packed as many belongings as I could get into my car and headed to Indiana!

The Reconciliation Attempt

All the way to Indiana, I went over several plans on how I was going to approach the situation, and how I thought those plans would play out. I did not even know if was being rational; I only knew, I had to try for my kids' sake! We needed each other in our lives; that, for sure, I did know!

Going over all my plans, reality would set in and I would have to pull over several times, due to the overwhelming emotion that would come over me! I remember one of those stops; it was around Bowling Green, KY, and I was weeping profusely, feeling sorry for myself. I came within a heart's beat of turning around and going back to Arkansas. I thought why my kids would want me around them; a half crazy man reliving a war in his mind every day and being drunk most of the time. What good would I be to them? I would probably be more of a liability on them than an asset for them. Then I realized that I was more than likely going to lose this battle, but I would rather lose it trying than not trying at all! I regained my composure and continued on.

When I arrived in Elwood, IN, I rented a room from a nice old lady for twenty dollars a week. She said she furnished breakfast five days a week for thirty-five dollars a week, but I declined the offer; that is why I paid so little. The following day I bought a paper and started looking for work. On my first attempt I hit pay dirt at a place called Marsh's Supermarket in a place called Tipton, about nine miles from Elwood. The store manager told me to return on Wednesday, and if my references checked out in Arkansas, I would be put to work on that day. Well, I went to work as a grocery stock clerk.

The holiday season was getting ready to start in a few days, and I had talked Sherry into allowing me to see the kids. She would bring them over once a week. Then it became twice a week, always when Mary Ruth (her mother) was working, attending to other duties away from home. She said that her mother did not know about the visits and it had to stay that way, or she might be kicked out of the house. I told her we could get a place of our own, but she would not have that. Worth a try, right!

As fate would have it, her mother did find out, and Sherry had hell to pay! DJ came to the rescue; he started crying, wanting his daddy to come to their house and live! Mary Ruth gave in to my son, and I was permitted to come to their house to visit with the kids in the evening three days a week for two hours. While I was grateful for this privilege, I did not like being watched like a hawk!

On the day after Thanksgiving, 1972, I was allowed to move in with them. Sherry said she had thoughts of wanting to get back together, and I thought that my plan was for reconciliation was beginning to work. I had not had a drink since I left Arkansas, and I thought things were going to work out; however, I knew that being a full-time boarder was the wrong move, but I did it anyway. I made the decision based on my emotions of being close to the kids every day. I had gone against my plan, and I felt it when I was moving in.

After I got settled in, I was told that I could not sit in the den with everyone else, but in the living room. I was also told that if I wanted anything to eat before I went to work, I could only eat buttered toast and was not to make coffee because it would wake everyone up. Every day, I was verbally abused, called everything in the book, physically hit, or shoved; I had hurt a lot of people physically for doing a lot less! I took and took just about all I could take!

On the December 28, Mary Ruth and Sherry were at the kitchen sink washing dishes. I went into the kitchen pantry to feed the dog, which was one of my chores. I noticed that the dog food was not there and asked where it was; Sherry said, "I don't know. Mom, where is the dog food?" Mary Ruth whirled around with a large knife in her hand and threw it, missing me by only inches! As she threw the knife, she said to me, "If you had looked in the first place, you would not have to ask, you stupid idiot!" I rose up, looked at the knife she threw which was stuck into the wall, grabbed the knife, and started toward Mary Ruth. Sherry said, "Don, don't do it!

Please don't do it!" Mary Ruth turned around and looked at me and looked scared, and let out a scream when she saw I was coming at her with the knife. When I was only about three feet from her, I raised the knife and said, "You're not worth it! None of you are worth it!" I looked at Sherry and continued, "Sherry, if you want to stay with this bitch, you go ahead! The two of you deserve one another! If you stay around each other long enough, maybe the two of you will be put out of your misery, by killing each other! I'm out of here!" Dale (Sherry's father) told me I needed to leave. I went into Sherry's bedroom, grabbed what things I could in a five-minute period, kissed the kids, and told DJ that I was leaving for awhile. On the way out I looked at Dale and said, "Putting up with that crap you put up with, you must be the most miserable man in the world!" Then I left the house. After that skirmish, I stayed in town a couple of days. I tried to call Sherry several times, but Mary Ruth would answer the phone. Finally when I called, Sherry answered the phone, and I asked if I could see the kids? She refused; and when I asked if I could talk to DJ on the phone, she also refused! She informed me very derogatorily that she had already explained it to him and not to worry about it, and that a restraining order was brought against me, and that I should get the hell out of Indiana; then she hung up.

When I left town, on New Year's Day, 1973, heading back to Arkansas, I felt dejected and defeated. In the past, I told myself, I could quit drinking any time I wanted to; I didn't need anyone or anybody, and I sure didn't need a head shrink! As I was driving, I knew then, I had been wrong about a lot of things; I had been right on some as well. The problem was, I was so messed up in the head that I didn't know the wrong from the right! I had lost my self-respect and my respect for others; my word was no good; everyone had lost faith in me, and I didn't have faith in myself. I could feel everyone talking about me and laughing at me, as if I were the scum of the earth; and maybe I was!

It seems that when you are by yourself driving down the road, you think of other ways to solve the problems at hand. All the ways I thought of I had already tried, and failed. When I thought of Donnie and Mark, I would break down crying and have to stop, because I couldn't see how to drive. I couldn't imagine a life without my kids in it; I also knew that in my state of mind (with what little ability I had left to rationalize), I would be more of a liability for them than an asset. I made a decision that I was going to really try to pull myself together, and maybe one day, I would be that asset they needed! What I didn't realize then was that getting my kids back was only part of the problem. The big problem was that I was in the battle for my life, and I was losing that battle. If I didn't win, my life would be over!

God, Please Help Me

Crossing the Mississippi River from Memphis, I wasn't singing; I was busy trying to put together a plan to win my kids back. I would go to the National Guard Armory and transfer back into the Arkansas Guard from the Indiana Guard. I would go back to Bill Willkie, and ask for my old job back again. Then I would rent a place to live, if Mom and Dad wouldn't let me stay with them for a while. Then no matter what, I would stop my drinking!

Everything went according to plan, except for one thing; I stopped drinking for only about two weeks. Then I thought that's all right, as long as I don't drink too much, and not let it interfere with my daily activities, and work; everything will be okay! That's like telling a politician to be honest; it isn't going to happen! Back then, as much as I had screwed up, I thought I had a handle on it!

A month later, Bill told me I was going to have to quit coming in drunk or he was going to have to let me go; I told him that I would save him the trouble, so I quit! Same thing happened with I don't know how many jobs within that year. I had developed a pattern; work until they confronted me about the problem, then run away! I was becoming unemployable! I suppose I had worked for just about every grocery store in town!

After a month and a half of looking for a job and being turned down, I was running out of money and didn't know where else to go or what to do; so I did what I did best; I took my last forty dollars and went to the nearest bar and started drinking. When it was closing time, the bartender told me I had to leave. I got into my car and started driving home, but Bryant was in the opposite direction to where I was going! When I realized it, I saw a road sign that said Russellville, which was about ninety miles west of Bryant! I turned around and decided to try it again; I was driving fast, and fell asleep at the wheel from drunkenness and hit a road sign, demolishing my car, breaking the windshield from the sign collapsing on my car, and my head hitting the windshield; my head was cut and bleeding from the impact! I wound up in the median; so I got out of the car and started walking down the median of the freeway, not even knowing where I was! It was raining cats and dogs; I fell down in a deep rut (more like a ditch) on the wet muddy ground. I started calling for help, but no one heard or saw me. Then I became overwhelmed with fear, an intense fear I had never known before; so intense that I felt I wasn't going to live through this ordeal, and I started crying for help again; and I hoped *he* would hear me! *God, help me! God, please help me; please*!

The rain had sobered me up; I was soaked and wet and cold; oh so cold! It started to rain harder, and each drop that hit me felt like a needle that penetrated deep into my skin! I cradled myself in a fetal position, hoping to warm myself, and shed some of the rain. I don't know how long I was in that ditch until a passing motorist stopped. He came over to me and asked if I was all right. I told him, no; and I asked him to take me to the VA Hospital in North Little Rock. He did, because he was on his way there too, to work!

He opened his trunk and took out a blanket, wrapped it around me, and then helped me into his car. He started talking to me, but I can't remember what he said because I passed out; the next thing I remember was that I was lying in a hospital bed asking where I was? The nurse told me, "You are in the VA Hospital in North Little Rock, AR. You have had an accident; a passing motorist brought you here at your request. The doctor will be in to talk with you in a few minutes." While waiting for the doctor, I wandered what everyone thought of me; I wondered what would become of me and if I was beyond help. Would they even help me? I thought maybe I should leave; that I was crazy for asking to be brought here in the first place! I attempted to sit up, but lay back down because I was so dizzy.

The doctor came in, introduced himself, and asked how my accident happened? I told him the best I could up until the Good Samaritan came. He asked me how much I had to drink; and was I drinking at the time of the accident? He asked me if I was an alcoholic. I told him that I didn't think so; then I changed my mind and said, "Yes, I believe I am; oh, I don't know; I only know I need help!" The doctor listened carefully as I tried to explain myself.

I was admitted to the alcoholic unit, where I spent thirty days drying out, getting therapy for my drinking problem. That was the first of three times I was in the VA Hospital in the year of 1973, all for drinking-related problems. In 1974, I was admitted twice to the psych unit, and again in September 1975. I spent my thirtieth birthday there. As I resisted drinking, the dreams would come back, and then while I was awake, I would imagine in my mind that I was still in Vietnam. I was becoming institutionalized, and I knew it. I was told by my Psychiatrist that I would not leave the hospital for a long time. I was given medications for hallucinations; they didn't help! All they did was render me harmless to other people, and I walked around like a zombie! For two weeks, I pretended to take my medication, and when the nurse would go to the next patient, I would spit them out in my hand and throw them away. One day I got caught; but I still refused to take it, and they put me in restraints! I had a session with my doctor a couple of days after the incident, and I remember the conversation went something like this; the doctor started the conversation:

"I understand you have been refusing to take your medication, Don. Is this true?" I told him that it was true, and the reason I did not want to take the pills is because they didn't help. "If you don't think they are helping you, why didn't you say something to us?"

I told him, "Because I don't want any medication! How in the hell do you think anyone can work on their problems all doped up?" "Those medications are to help you, Don." "Doctor, please, just for two weeks, take me off all my meds and let me try and deal with my problems without them! If you see that I am not better, you can put me back on them, and I will accept the way I am and not bring the matter up again, okay?" The doctor was silent for what seemed like a lifetime, and then he spoke, "Don, have you ever played golf?" I told him, no, and said, "What does this have to do with my wanting to be taken off medication?" "Why haven't you played golf?" I responded, "Well, it's a little dumb, don't you think, to hit a little white ball and then run after it just to hit it again?" "What sport did you play when you were a kid?" "Baseball is my game!" "Were you good at it?" "Yes, state champs in 1961!" The doctor continued, "Golf is a little like baseball; you use a bat to hit a baseball, and you use a club to hit a golf ball; they both are an extension of the body. When you hit a baseball you run and try to make it safely before someone throws it back. In golf, you hit the ball and go get it until you put it in a hole. Not much difference, except for one thing. In baseball, the outcome of the game is decided by how well nine men have played; and in golf, the outcome of the game depends on you and you alone! Some will not play because they are afraid of failing, and some play to try and overcome their failures! Some play because it is a challenge; people play for all kinds of reasons. My point is this: I do not believe you have given up. I believe you have a lot of will, and I believe that after our session today, you will find yourself; not today, or next week, but eventually I believe you will, and that is why I am going to order all medications halted for three weeks, and I am going to grant your request and write an order for your therapy to be on the hospital golf course two sessions per day for at least one hour each session. I want you to do your best. Will you do that if I proceed with taking you off your medication?" I told him "yes, sir" and continued, "I don't know the rules or where to hit the ball. Is someone going to teach me the rules and where to hit the ball?" The doctor told me, "Don't worry about the rules now, just learn to hit the ball, son; just learn to hit the ball." "That shouldn't be too hard, doc; I used to hit homeruns!" The doc said,

"That's great! Maybe you will hit another one. I will see you in three weeks." At the time of that session, I didn't understand what he meant by hitting another homerun; we were talking about golf. I didn't ask; I was just glad I was off all that medication!

CHAPTER SIXTEEN

A Little Harder Than I Thought

The next morning after breakfast, I walked across the street to the Caddy House and handed the Special Services attendant the order that my doctor had written. The attendant handed me a bag, with five or six clubs and about a dozen golf balls. I asked him why I needed so many balls; I was only supposed to hit one! He said, "You have never played golf before, have you?" I told him, no, I haven't. He said, you will find out; and when you run out, come back and I will give you some more! I asked him, "Are you trying to be funny; because if you are, you need to take the funny course in school over!" He looked at me and smiled, then said, "Have a good game." I told him, thank you, and went to the first tee where I laid a ball on the ground and took out the biggest club in the bag. I didn't know one club from another back then, but I figured the bigger the club, the heavier. I had every intention of knocking the cover off that golf ball! I teed the ball (I knew that because I would watch the other guys do it) and took aim with the club, and swung as hard as I could; not only did I miss the ball, but I also lost my balance and fell flat on my ass! My first thought was to look around to see if anyone might have seen my clown act; then I looked and that little white ball was still sitting on that tee, as I had placed it! I got up and took aim, then swung again (just as hard as I could), and missed again, *but I didn't fall down*! I figured, I must be doing something right, because I was still on my feet! Then I thought, I must have a bad club, so I got another one out of my bag. I took aim for a third time, and again swung as hard I could; and I hit the ball. I actually hit the ball! It went about twenty feet! Even though I hit the ball, I wasn't satisfied, so I picked the ball up and teed it up again. I was going to approach the ball for a fourth time, when I heard someone behind me say, "A little harder than you thought?" It was the caddy attendant; I said, "What am I doing wrong?" He said, "Everything! Just keep your eye on the ball, and don't swing so hard!" I did as he suggested, and to my surprise the ball sailed well over a hundred yards; it landed on the far side of another fairway, but at least I hit the ball. I was going to go get the ball, then I remembered; I have more balls! I walked down about a hundred yards or so and placed a ball on the fairway. I finally landed on the green after about twenty or so strokes! My goal was to beat those twenty or so strokes on the next hole; but it didn't happen!

For the next five or six days, that's the way my golf game was! After the third day, I was determined not to be defeated by that little white ball. I would get so frustrated and upset with myself; I cursed a blue streak up and down the fairways, on the greens, in the rough, in the water! The more I screwed up, the more useless and frustrated I became with myself; and on the seventh day of playing this stupid game, everything finally came to a head, and I couldn't tolerate myself or anyone else!

Miracle on the Golf Course

I threw my bag and clubs as far as I could; they scattered everywhere. I sat down by a pine tree, looked up toward heaven, started a conversation with God that would last for over two hours, and said, "God, You are the cause of this! You are the cause of all my problems! You are never around when I need You; what good are You! Why don't You write me off! I'm no good anyway! I have hurt everyone I came into contact with; no one trusts me anymore, not even my parents (I had gotten up to pick up my clubs and put them back into the bag, and was walking around), and God, You don't even care anymore (by this time, I was weeping so hard I could hardly talk)! If you did, you would do something about it! You won't even answer me; that's the kind of God you are! *Why don't you answer me*!"

All of a sudden after talking and cursing God for about an hour and a half, a profound weakness came over me and I fell to the ground; I tried to get up several times, but could not! I was crying so hard then that not only were tears still streaming down, but saliva was also running out of my mouth! I heard a voice from deep within (up until now, I was the only one speaking), as God spoke, "I have always been here, and have protected you, just as I said I would!" "I need to get up! Why can't I get up!" "Forgive yourself so I can help you!" "I can't; I have hurt too many people and made a mess of my life; how can I forgive myself when you won't even forgive me!" "I have always forgiven you, but it is you who needs to forgive yourself!" "I don't know if I can, Lord! Will you give me the strength to do it!" You have always had the strength within your heart. "You have the choice of free will!" "Lord I still don't know if I can forgive myself, but I will surely try my best. I will surely try!" "*Then I shall do the rest, my son*!" Suddenly, I felt an overwhelming burst of energy! I rose to my feet and returned to my dormitory; I lay down on my bunk and with tear-filled eyes fell off to sleep. I awakened the following morning feeling refreshed! I really believe it was the best night's sleep I have ever had; and I had the most wonderful feeling of calmness within myself, something I had not felt since I was a child.

At that exact time in my life, I felt a warmness and complete serenity, no torment of horrors of the war in my mind, and an inner strength; and I felt the bitterness and the hate toward myself and everyone else go away, and the calmness within me; it was so serene! The best way I can explain it is that it was like looking out over the ocean, and as far as you can see it is a perfect sea of water with no waves or ripples, like a sea of glass! I knew that I knew my soul had been saved by the grace of God! It was then I felt that everything was going to be all right! I rose to my feet and shouted at the top of my lungs, "I'm saved, I'm saved, I'm saved. Thank God, I'm saved!"

The nursing staff came running into the sleeping quarters and thought I was hallucinating; they thought that I thought I was Jesus or something! I raised my hands to shoulder height and said, "I'm okay, Mr. Benson. Believe me, I am just fine! In fact, I don't believe I have been finer in my entire life!" "Are you sure you are okay!" "Do I look okay to you, Benson?" "Yes, you look okay; what has gotten into you, Reeves!" "God's love has gotten into me. I have been saved! You do know what saved me, don't you, Benson!" Mr. Benson put his hands on his hips and commented, "Lord, have mercy. It's a miracle! You better get to breakfast, Don; the chow hall closes in about ten minutes; now that your soul has been fed, it's time to feed your face!"

The next day, word spread throughout the unit staff, and they all came and talked with me. Three days later, my doctor summoned me to his office.

"Don, how is the golf therapy going?"

"Great, sir! When I first tried hitting the ball, I couldn't believe it was so hard. I became so frustrated I wanted to quit! Then two days ago, I asked Mr. Burrows at the caddy house to give me a lesson on how to hit the ball, and I am hitting it pretty good now. I believe I am going to like this game!"

"Don, do you remember the last thing I said to you, during our last session, about hitting another homerun?"

"Yes, sir, I do!"

"Well, I believe you have done it! In fact you have made remarkable progress in the past ten days! In fact, it is miraculous, so much that I am going to move you to a step down unit, and if all goes well over the next two weeks, I am going to recommend you for discharge! How does that sound to you?"

"That sounds great, Doctor. I believe I am ready now!"

"In two weeks, I want to observe you a little longer. You just keep hitting homeruns!"

"Oh, haven't you heard, doc? I've graduated. I am rolling golf balls in a hole now!"

"I will see you in two weeks, Don."

"Doctor, I can never thank you enough for what you have done for me. You did not have to take a chance on me the way you did, and I am very grateful. One of these days, I hope I can repay you."

"The only payment I want from you is for you to have a happy and productive life. Now go and roll some balls in the hole!"

"I will, sir. You can count on it!"

The next two weeks, I was on the golf course working on anger management three to four hours every day. The rest of the day, I spent my time at the Hospital Library reading as much about Jesus Christ as I could.

Three days before I was discharged from the hospital, I opened my Bible at random; and there, staring me in the face, was the scripture, Philippians, 4:13; I can do all things through Christ which strengthens me. I shouted, "Yes, I can!" There is power in those words! If you don't believe me, say them aloud to yourself, with meaning several times. You will be beside yourself with excitement! This is the scripture that I always remember when things get me down. I always get refreshed when I say these words aloud; I can do *all* things through Christ which strengthens me!

Positive Thinking vs. Negative Thinking

You could fill a library with the thousands of books and pamphlets about the way people think and why. I have read more than my share of them, rehabilitating myself, in my three semesters in college studying Marketing and Sales Psychology, in nursing in-services, in the many sales seminars attended, and sales psychology courses I have had the privilege of attending. I could probably teach a seminar on the effects of positive thinking. I know I could on the effects of negative thinking, something I was pretty much an authority on!

One writer will tell us, if we think negative, we do negative things. Another will tell us that as we think about an undertaking before we start it, so shall the results of that task be accordingly. If we think positive things, we receive positive results, and vice versa. A positive person sees the glass half full, but the negative person sees it half empty! It is not what you say about the glass; it is what you first think about the glass when you first see it!

We live in a negative world of clichés. Why are traffic lights called stop lights? If we were positive about traffic lights, shouldn't they be called go lights? The weatherman tells us there is a thirty percent chance of rain, when a seventy percent chance of sunshine is a lot more positive. We even tell ourselves there is a forty percent chance that I can't do a task, when there is a sixty percent chance you will; and since the computer age has come upon us, some one coined the phrase: garbage in, garbage out! Even the Bible tells us we are the product of our own thinking; "For as he thinks in his heart, so is he." Proverbs, 23:7.

Psychologists tell us that between the age of four to six, our personality, and habits of the way we think are pretty much set in stone, and that is the way we will view life. They also tell us, the personality is there to stay for the most part, but we can reprogram our way of thinking. They are easy tasks to perform;, however, they do require constant repetition and strong self-discipline. I know this to be a fact, because I am a product of reprogramming. It is not very difficult to achieve when you have a good mind-set; and when I say I am a product, I am in no way a master of the art. On the other hand, I believe I have come a long way from those bad years of battle fatigue (acute PTSD) and the negative thinking it caused!

According to Webster's Dictionary, the word "Repent" means to change one's mind. When I was on that golf course pleading and cursing God, and after several hours, gave in to His will; I repented of my wrongdoings and my negative way of thinking; in other words, I changed my mind! That does not mean, I became perfect; oh, far from it!

When I repented of my sins and was reborn, I was forgiven from the things I had done. It does not mean that my memory was erased from them and/or that my negative way of thinking would somehow miraculously change in the blink of an eye!

As the old sayings go, old habits are hard to break, but they can be broken with constant awareness and discipline. I found this out the hard way; getting my drinking under control was much harder than I thought it would be. I was hearing a hundred voices in my mind saying, one drink won't hurt; while only one was telling me not to do it! As Jesus said on the Mount of Olives, when he found the Disciples asleep, after he rose from praying, "The spirit is willing but the flesh is weak." God always knows the exact appointed time to send someone to the rescue; her name was Sylvia, and her two children, Michael and Lori! "It is not good that man should be alone; I will make him a help meet for him." (Gen. 2:18)

"The Pretty Lady"

She was the most beautiful woman I had ever seen, and I had to introduce myself; well, let me back up a little. I'm getting ahead of myself.

I had taken a job in a furniture factory in Benton, AR, where my mother worked. I was assigned to the drawer assembly line. Sylvia was one position up from me; she stapled the drawers together, after the person in front of her glued them together. They were sent down to me, and I would sand the joints and send them on down the line for finishing. Sylvia and I would eye each other during the work process for the first couple of days, but did not speak to each other; however, I sure did want to, and I thought she wanted me to.

At lunch break on my second day of work, I asked my mother who the girl stapling the drawers was. I remember my mother's response verbatim, "You don't want to have anything to do with her. She is the boss's pet, and besides that, she ain't nothin' but a little you-know-what!" Now sometimes my mother jumps to conclusions before she checks things out and assumes her thoughts to be fact! "Mama, how do you know that?" "Because I talked to her about it!" "You mean, you accused her of being the boss's pet, and she went off on you because it probably isn't true! Now, isn't that right, Mom?" "Oh, she is the boss's pet all right, she always gets her way!" "Mom, do you think the boss is trying to play up to her; attractive women in a place like this, there are always going to be men hitting on them. That doesn't make them bad; just popular. Besides, the boss is not only about two French fries short of a Happy Meal, he looks like road kill!" "Well son, you do what you want to do, but I am telling you, that woman is trouble!" "Mom, I know you mean well, but I think you are reading her wrong. I am going to introduce myself and find out for myself."

On the afternoon break, I went to where she hung out and introduced myself; and she introduced herself, and our conversation barely got off the ground, before it was time to go back to work. On the way back to our work station, I asked her if she would like to go out to lunch with me the next day, and she accepted.

The next day, Sylvia asked me if I knew the lady that put the faces on the drawers! I told her, "Yes, why do you ask?" "I saw you hanging around her at lunch yesterday. I don't like her!" "Well, she told me about the job opening here, and she was the only person I knew here at the time. Why don't you like her?" "She accused me of being the boss's pet, which is totally untrue! That old man has been hitting on me for the last three weeks. I didn't want to say anything to him for fear of getting fired!" "And you went off on her and told her in so many words where to go, right?" "How did you know?" "She told me; and she also told me to stay away from you, that you were trouble." "I'm going to give her another piece of my mind. You just wait until we get back to the plant!" "Take it easy; relax, Sylvia; that woman is always jumping to conclusions. It's her nature. She told me those things because she thought she was protecting me!" "Protecting you!" "Yes, she is my mother!" "Your mother!" "Yep." "Well, she is going to have to change her attitude toward me before I will talk to her again!" "You just leave that task to me, Pretty Lady; I will take care of it!"

I was leaving in twelve days for Fort McCoy, WS, for four weeks of school with my Army National Guard unit, and I wanted to convince Mom she was wrong about Sylvia; I also wanted to see as much of "The Pretty Lady" as I could before I left for McCoy.

When I told Mom the story of how the boss was hitting on her, she calmed down a bit. I told Mom, I knew she was a good person, and to give her a chance because I was going to ask her out. She agreed to call a truce and observe for my sake.

I did not know if I was ready for another relationship or not, so I approached the situation with caution; I did not want to get hurt again like before, and I sure didn't want to hurt her.

Through the several dates we had prior to my deployment to Fort McCoy, I found out she had come off an abusive marriage and had two children: a ten-year-old boy and a three-year-old little girl. I realized, Sylvia was not only the prettiest woman I had ever met on the outside, but ten times more beautiful within, and a devout Christian. I thought to myself, I was not deserving of her and even though I wanted to be with her, I was glad to be leaving; it would give me time to think about the situation. It was really love at first sight, and we were inseparable, but this feeling of inadequacy continued to build up inside me; and I was telling myself, I was not good enough for her. What if the dreams come back; and the hallucinations? How would she handle that? It would be too much for her. What if I can't get total control of my drinking problem? I was making progress, but still had a long way to go. What if I can't give her the things she wants and needs? What if I continue to be a total, miserable failure! All these questions came to mind, and I knew I had to find the answers, but even more, I made known these questions to "The Pretty Lady," and also of my inadequacies. They had to be addressed before we were to move on with our relationship. For me, it would have to be a 100 percent commitment on my part; my love for her must be unconditional, or not at all, and with all the baggage I had been carrying around all those years dragging me down, I did not know if I could do that! On the other hand, I knew God had brought us together, and He had a plan for us! Would we surrender to God's will or not? We both had a mountain of things to think about, and a lot of questions to answer, while we were apart from each other!

Upon my return from Fort McCoy, Wisconsin, I was afraid Sylvia would have considered me a liability more than an asset, so I waited for her to contact me, instead of contacting her. She knew the date I would return, and after three days, I figured she had blown me off. It was just as well, because I really felt, if we didn't make it, the hurt would start all over again for both of us. I was not sure I was the person she needed; a special person like her deserved someone who was already established in life and knew where he was going. I didn't have a clue as to what I wanted to do, other than the fact that I loved her more than life itself! I felt overwhelmed; my heart ached and yearned for her so much! I was way over my head with this wonderful, beautiful woman, and I hoped and prayed that she did not feel the same way I did!

I turned back to an old habit and got drunk; in the middle of that process, I told myself, I did not want to go down that hard road again and decided to check in at the VA for alcohol rehab again. Two weeks went by while at the VA, when I had a visitor; I told no one of my tenure there (not even my parents), but somehow Sylvia found me. I was doing something I was not good at; I was on the golf course trying to hit that little white ball. When I saw her, I tried to hide, because I was ashamed of her seeing me there. She assured me that it was all right, and she told me she loved me, and together we would work though both of our problems. She told me, there is no problem too big for God, if we put him first in our life; she was right! With God's help and the wonderful woman He brought into my life, I surrendered unconditionally over to love that day, her amazing love for me! God made a way to bring us together, and what God brings together stays together! That day I overcame my fears and was overwhelmed with joy in my heart! Two weeks later, I left the VA never to return as a psych patient again.

CHAPTER SEVENTEEN

Mr. and Mrs. Don Reeves and Family

We were married on December 11, 1976, at my parents' house. It was Michael, Lori, "The Pretty Lady," and me. I had a wife who loved me with all her heart. "The Pretty Lady" had a husband who loved her with all his heart and did not verbally abuse her, and Michael and Lori had a Dad that loved them with all his heart and did not abuse them! I had the greatest family in the world!

On May 6, 1978, a new addition to our great family arrived: Nick Patrick Reeves, named after the greatest man I have ever known, my grandfather. The only thing that would complete our family would be for Donnie and Mark to be with us; but until that happened, I would be happy, content, and blessed with my wonderful family.

I was driving a truck for Affiliated Foods, delivering goods to their independent grocer affiliates in the state of Arkansas at the time Nick was born. On May 6, 1978, I was en route to Jonesborough, Arkansas, delivering an eighteen wheeler load of milk. When I arrived, the dairy manager told me the news that the "Pretty Lady" was at the hospital in Benton and in labor! Nearly every employee at that store, including the owner, pitched in with the unloading so that I would not be delayed. All of us together unloaded that entire trailer full of milk in less than ten minutes! I engaged my emergency flashers and took off, stopping for nothing; I was going as fast as that truck would go! It is 155 miles back to Little Rock, and I made the trip in one hour and fifty-five minutes! I arrived at Saline Memorial Hospital at 2:15 p.m. to find that my son was already born; he had arrived three hours earlier.

The "Pretty Lady" was glad to see me, and I was relieved to know she was all right, and that our new born son was healthy! She told me that the nurses were asking her to name the baby, and she told them that they would have to wait until I arrived. I told her, "Nick Patrick will be his name," and she agreed. The legacy of my grandfather lives on with my son, and what a legacy it is!

Operation Christmas Tree

In June 1978, I accepted an assignment with the National Guard, as an active duty recruiter for a four-year tour. My best friend, Master Sergeant (MSG) Charlie Hass was my NCOIC, who had joined the R and R (Recruiting and Retention) force three years earlier and had worked his way up to the noncommissioned officer in charge of all of south Arkansas. He asked me if I would work for him, and I agreed to do so. It meant a lot more pay and an opportunity to continue my sales education at the Army's expense.

My friend, Charlie, and I had a very good working relationship. At work he was MSG Hass and I was Staff Sergeant (SSG) Reeves. There was never a time that friendship took precedence over work. After work, we were Charlie and Don again. Our friendship has stood the test of time of a span, up to this point, of sixty years, and we have always been there for each other in the bad and good times.

Charlie has always given me the most difficult assignments because he trusted me to put forth 100 percent effort in every task handed me and because of my quick study. The area he put me in was one in which all of his recruiters had failed to meet quota and the

R and R Commander was on him hard and heavy to put someone there that would get all of the Guard Units up to 100 percent within one year. I accepted the challenge believing I could accomplish the goal.

I had a four county responsibility: Garland, Clark, Grant, and Hot Spring. The main cities in those counties were: Hot Springs, which is where the national park is located; Arkadelphia, home to two Universities; Henderson State and Ouachita Baptist, where Governor Mike Hukabee graduated; Sheridan, mainly a logging and trucking town; Malvern, home town to Billy Bob Thornton and most importantly my "Pretty Lady." All these small cities were considerably difficult to recruit for obvious reasons; Hot Springs is a tourist city and a resort. Arkadelphia, a college town; most of the young people had their sights on going to a University somewhere and were not interested in the military. The good people of Sheridan just wanted to be left alone; and the Administrative Service Technician (AST), SFC George Scorch, ran a good unit and it stayed at 100 percent most of the time. All I had to do was make courtesy visits. The city of Malvern; well, it was the toughest of the four. Most of the town's people were anti-military because of the past reputation the guard unit there had.

Several years prior to my arriving, the members of the guard units, during drill, would sneak off during duty hours and go to Hot Springs and buy booze, come back to Malvern and drive around town drinking, and that didn't sit too well on the town folk, especially a small town of only 8,000, smack dab in the middle of the Bible belt. When I arrived, almost all of the members that bucked the system had either moved on or were kicked out. However for the majority of the city's population, the damage had been done and the unit's image was scared, to put it mildly. I told Charlie I needed to work on the community before I worked on recruiting, and that I needed time before I started producing in Malvern.

I concentrated on the Hot Springs and Arkadelphia units in order to make quota and also rubbed elbows with all the politicians in all my areas of responsibility; and by the middle of September I had come up with a plan to change the image of the Malvern unit. At that time, little did I know that I would be known around town as the recruiter who became the humanitarian.

I presented my idea to MSG Hass, and he told me that I was taking on too much, but I was determined to make it work. I went to the Malvern Unit AST, SSG James Taylor, who said no one in the unit would volunteer to help. I went to the Unit Commander, CPT DuPrey, and he said, "I think it's crazy, idiotic, and a lot of hard work." Everyone I talked with was against my idea, but also told me if I wanted to do it on my own I could. That did not discourage me from implementing my plan; and on October 1, 1978, the first annual Operation Christmas Tree was launched.

The plan was to put flyers up in businesses, on light poles, and anywhere else I could get permission. I put ads in the local paper, also PSA (Public Service Advertising), at the local radio station, announcing that the Malvern unit of the Arkansas National Guard would be taking donations in good condition for clothes and toys; also non-perishable food items. The donations would be assorted out according to each individual child and family need, and distributed to the needy in the city of Malvern and Hot Spring County in time for Christmas.

The first ten days I was totally on my own; within two weeks the Malvern NG unit was frontpage news receiving all sorts of toys, from bicycles to teddy bears, and clothes of all different apparel and sizes, and the food—*wow*! I have never seen such outpouring of giving; it was tremendous; I never expected a response of that magnitude! Most of the people who donated went to all the active duty personnel in the armory and thanked them for what they were doing! I did not tell the townspeople that I was the only volunteer at that time. After all, I was doing it for an ulterior motive; at least it started out that way. Then I saw the people caring, and the needy folks who came in crying for their children, and my unit counterparts saw it too! I started getting soldiers in the office wanting to volunteer, and by the first of December, I was able to turn the entire operation over to the unit; however, I continued to assist. It was quite a sight. The soldiers seemed to have a sense of purpose, a reason to be proud of who they were, and excited with anticipation at seeing a child's face light up when they would give them their gifts, or a grateful mom and/or dad with tears in their eyes when they would be able to have Christmas dinner!

It has been said many times and in many ways, "If you want to be a success, help others succeed." They may not thank you for it at the time of that help, but they will never forget you and what you did for them. Nothing is more heartwarming than to see the happiness on a child's face; that image will be forever imbedded in your memory. Oh, what memories I had of that event!

Christmas of 1978 was good for sixty-six families in Hot Spring County and for me as well, with good feelings of helping someone. When that first Operation Christmas Tree was over, it did not seem to matter much where I helped to create a better image for the guard unit in Malvern (although it did happen); what did matter was that I did not get discouraged when everyone told me I was crazy. If I had scrubbed that mission of 1978, there might not have been other guard units around the state of Arkansas and this great country who have helped their community like Malvern did; and in 2008 nationally, there would have been over 755,000 children and families without a Christmas! I would like to believe I had a part in making that happen!

The Malvern unit continued Operation Christmas Tree another three years, although they renamed it Operation Santa Claus; it was more successful each year. Oh, I might also state that the Malvern National Guard Unit is now one of the most respected and strongest units in the nation!

Fifteen other units in the state of Arkansas also adopted similar programs; it became contagious and other states adopted their own programs, and as of 2010, over two thousand National Guard units helped over one million families have a merry Christmas. It just goes to prove: "It only takes *one* person with *one* plan to help a *country*! Which *one* of 'you' will be the next *one*?"

Don Reeves the Salesman

I left the Army R and R Corps in 1982 and went back to being a parttime soldier in the National Guard at my old unit, "B" Company, 112th Signal Battalion, in Benton, AR, where I was assigned to Node center control as the Operations Sergeant.

I took a full-time position in sales for a home improvement company. While on the R and R force, I was given the opportunity to attend numerous civilian sales schools and courses which prepared me for a sales career. There would not be enough space on one page to list all the schools and courses and what they entailed that I attended; all of them together were equivalent to an associate degree in Marketing and Economics, plus Sales Psychology.

I traveled a lot and was away from home most of the time, living out of a suitcase and in motel rooms. It was this part of sales that was the hardest to get used to. Sometimes there would be slow periods, and I would have down time. By then, I had grown a lot in my faith in God, but still had a long way to go, as all of us do. I had gotten control of my drinking problem, so during the slow periods, I stayed busy reading my Bible in my room and preparing for church the upcoming Sunday. I had been elected as Sunday School Superintendent, and one of my duties was to start the main service. The Pretty Lady played the piano and we also led the song service. While in my motel room, it gave me the opportunity to prepare for my part of the service.

I made very good money in the home improvement industry. I broke several sales records, some of which still stand in the industry. I still did not like being away from my family all week though, but it was a living, so the Pretty Lady and I tolerated it. Then the bottom fell out of the industry in September 1986, and I started looking for another position and found it!

The Professional Education Center

In 1987, I took an active duty position with the National Guard Profession Education Center (NGPEC, or PEC) at Camp Robinson in North Little Rock, Arkansas. PEC received their orders from the National Guard Bureau at the Pentagon in Washington, DC.

The PEC was at that time the only school the Army National Guard had for MOS qualification, and may still be. It taught over sixty different MOSs (career fields) to over thirty-eight thousand soldiers annually.

I worked there in support of the school.

I worked directly for the Commander of the DOIM (Department of Information Management). I pulled double duty for Lieutenant Colonel (LTC) Walden as his administrative technician and his aide. In other words, I was his shadow; I prepared all of his paperwork, wrote department memos, advised him on his diplomacy, and assisted the LTC in department regulation; prepared and implemented the budget for the department, and submitted the entire school budget to the NGB (National Guard Bureau). I went everywhere he went, and was also his memory; that man was the most absent-minded person I have ever known. However, this was a good thing; it kept me working! The busier he got, the more he forgot, and it was SFC Reeves to the rescue! I kept up with everything, from paperclips to the plane tickets, for the flights we would have to make on military business. I took all his notes at meetings, and constantly reminded him of his daily schedule; but then, that's what an aide is supposed to do! He was one of the finest individuals I have had the pleasure of knowing throughout my military career; when he wanted to praise the department, for a job well done, he would do it, and do it great, but when he needed to get tough, he called on me to do it, sometimes to full bird colonels and generals. I don't believe he knew how to get tough. He had been an administrator his entire career, so playing the tough game was not his cup of tea. We were both left-brained (show me the facts type of individuals), and together, both of us would analyze and research before making any decision for the department. I suppose that is why we hit it off so well. The two of us became good friends, and it isn't very often that enlisted and officers pal around together in any branch of the service.

LTC Walden cried when giving a speech on my behalf, at my farewell ceremony! It was not until then I realized just how much of a difference I had made in his life. I know he made a difference in mine, just by being my friend.

When I left the DOIM in August 1990 to attend Army nursing school, I had to transfer to the Army Nurse Corps, and that meant going to another Unit, the 148th Evacuation Hospital (dissolved in 1998). I was maxed out in my rank, so I had to either stay where I was and be grandfathered, which meant retire in two years (which I didn't want) or find another slot in the position of First Sergeant (1SG). The 148th had that position, and my test scores were high enough to be accepted for nursing school, so I grabbed it! I also had lost a part of my hearing (high intensity), and could no longer stay in the signal corps with that hearing loss; it required listening to signal tones in a headset which I could not hear.

Mobilization to War, Again

I had gotten settled in the school setting once again and was doing quite well. I was enjoying learning how to be a nurse and the probability of helping people. Then on November 21, 1990, I was called out of class to the administration office; when I got to admin., I was told that I had a phone call. I picked up the receiver, and at the other end, it was my AST at the 148th. He told me that it was a Raging Bull alert, and for me and all of my counterparts in school to report to HQ immediately! That could only have meant one thing; I was going back to war, and the thought of that brought back a lot of sleeping dogs within me! I would rather have let them sleep longer! For the second time in my life, my country needed me in another war: the first time when I was eighteen, and again at the age of forty-five. It was different this time, unlike the first; the first time, I went into combat trained to take lives, and the second time to save lives. It made the burden a lot more bearable.

I hung the phone up and went back to class and told the other six soldiers the news, and we left class, not knowing if we would ever see our classmates again.

On the way to the Armory, I stopped and called home to tell Sylvia the news, and told her I would see her when I could.

Arrival at the armory was chaotic; all kinds of rumors were floating around; a meeting of all Platoon Commanders, Platoon Sergeants, and Section Leaders was to be held at 1400 hours that day, and the official word would come down.

We received the word in the meeting that we were mobilized as of that day (Wednesday, November 21, 1990). All leaves were canceled, and no one was to leave the compound without permission. It was suggested to the commander that monthly drill be scheduled for the upcoming weekend, and to let the troops off, and bring them back in Friday; it would give them a day and a half to get their personal gear in order, and time with their families; and permission was granted. Formation was held for all 470 personnel, and everyone was to report back on Friday, the twenty-third. However, all Platoon Commanders, Platoon Sergeants, and Section Leaders, myself included, did not have that luxury. We stayed until 1700 hours for briefings, and reported in the next day as well, pre-planning meetings and laying fingers on equipment that had to be packed up.

Ten days later we found ourselves at our mobilization station in Ft. Polk, LA, where we would be calling home prior to deploying to the Middle East.

Meanwhile, back at Camp Robinson, a JAG Officer was investigating the mobilization of all the personnel that were attending nursing school. It seems we were not supposed to be pulled out of school and were to return. After arguments between the Army and the

JAG Corps, the JAG Corps won the argument and I, along with my six soldiers and eleven others, were released back to our orders to return to school. That happened on the December 26, 1990.

When we returned to school, our head nursing instructor was kind enough to allow us to get caught up on what we had missed. Christmas break was going on, and we missed several vital sections of our schooling, including semester exams. She worked with us during Christmas break and allowed us to take semester exams.

Meanwhile at Ft. Polk, our unit left for the Middle East on New Year's Day, 1991. They would be combined with other military hospital units to form a Combined Armed Services Hospital (*cash*), and returned back home on May 6, 1991. I, along with my counterparts, graduated from nursing school in the month of June 1991.

CHAPTER EIGHTEEN

The Senior Years

After nursing school, I would stay in the Guard only another four years; on August 18, 1995, I retired from Military Service, ending thirty years of honorable service. I was happy to retire, and I had given my country more than they asked of me; but I was sad and went into a mild depression knowing I had to leave something I cherished so much. But as my wife always does, she saw me through it all and I settled in to a full-time civilian setting.

I worked in a few area hospitals, in a hospice care setting, and Geri-Psych, and in 1997 gave up nursing on a full-time basis and went back into sales, working in the home improvement industry and as a mortgage loan officer. I had some success in the field, but not like before. I worked for two mortgage companies, and both went bankrupt shortly after I went to work. I decided to leave that business, because going bankrupt was not what I had in mind.

I was in between jobs on September 11, 2001, when I awakened to see on the TV what I thought was an action movie; my mom was staying with us then, recuperating from surgery. I asked her what she was watching, and she looked at me with tears in her eyes and said, "Terrorists hijacked planes and crashed them into the World Trade Center; all those people dead, so bad, oh so bad!" I sat down beside her to comfort her, telling her everything was going to be all right, even though I knew that day our world would change for the worst. I told Mom that those people who died were in God's hands. I woke the Pretty Lady and told her what had happened.

Everyone knows exactly where they were and what they were doing when the twin towers and the Pentagon were attacked, just as the generation before us did when Pearl Harbor was attacked by the Japanese.

Yes, 9/11 was indeed a sad day in our nation's history, one that will not be forgotten; those pictures will be etched in our memory throughout our lives and for generations to come.

I lost Dad on the September 21, 1994, and Mom on March 3, 2009. There are only three of my mother's siblings left out of nine, and none on my father's side. Most of the friends I grew up with have gone on to be with the Lord. Charlie and Richard are still with us, and the three of us continue to be the best of friends, though Charlie and I are in contact with each other more often.

My Soul Mate

I have been fortunate to have the most wonderful woman share my life for thirty-five years and counting; if we are so lucky as to live another thirty-five years, I still would not have enough time to properly express the love I have for this woman. She has been my rock, my reason for going on, the glue that has held me together; her understanding of my problems from the war and the disappointments that life brings us, sometimes on a regular basis, has been unchanging. Her kind heart for others has only gotten larger with time, and there is not a day that goes by that she does not have a kind word for the people she meets and sees along the way; she always looks for the good in others, regardless of the mistakes they have made in the past.

Her determination and focus on enjoying life has kept her young at heart, and beautiful, not only in my eyes, but in everyone who meets her. Her devotion to our children and ten grandchildren is amazing; and her devotion to me has been phenomenal, and my love for her continues to grow and flourish as each day goes by.

We have never gone to sleep, mad at each other; if we have a discussion, and it lingers on, before we go to bed we call a truce and pick it back up the following day. We use this time to think about the gravity of the situation, and most of the time we find that our disagreement wasn't worth discussing in the first place. We have never shouted at each other in anger; when we married, we became a union of one. If you shout at your spouse, you are shouting at yourself, and you don't like to be shouted at, even if it is you doing the shouting! After all, look at the person your spouse married!

Her faith in God and our Lord and Savior, Jesus Christ, is impeccable, and seeing her faith in action has helped me to grow in mine. Our marriage from day one has had Christ at the head of our marriage and family; it really does take three to make a successful and healthy relationship. Without Him, we would be a couple of wandering souls, making guesses as to what to do next!

My wife has helped me through the Battle Fatigue from the war (now called PTSD), which triggered psychological alcoholism, the darkest times of my life,; some in which she hurt in her soul as much as I did. Most would have given up, but she never faltered or wavered; she remained lovingly devoted. Her loving and caring approach to the past and present problems and difficulties has always succeeded. To quote her, "Love will always win in the end; always!"

I will forever be thankful to God for rescuing me with this wonderful woman. I found hope in her hope, courage to face my fears in her strength; I found integrity through her unwavering duty to do the right thing; I found faith in her faith, steadfastness in her undying spirit that says, never give up! All these things I had, and thought I lost but found they were deeply imbedded within me; this amazing woman helped me retrieve them. There is one thing I never knew though, and that is unconditional love, until this amazing lady, through her actions, her caring and undying love for me, showed me; for this I am eternally grateful to "My Pretty Lady!"

SUMMARY

After several sales positions from 1997 to mid 2001, in January 2002, I became an independent contract courier and have just recently retired. The "Pretty Lady" retires at the end of this year (2011), and we plan to travel the country as much as possible, while we still have our health to enjoy it.

When I entered the Marines, I was seventeen years old; it seems like only a short time ago. I gave the Marines all I had; it was very demanding. It took all the mental and physical energy I could muster, from boot camp to the last day in Vietnam, and I loved every minute of living on the edge! There were times when I did not know if I was going to make it back on some of those missions; most of them were in areas we and only three or four other people knew about.

I participated in six major campaigns, had twelve sniper missions, nine search and seek missions, fifteen search and destroy missions, and over two hundred patrol and ambush missions, thirty of which were long range. I lost two of my friends on two separate missions: Jimmy Hatfield, and Tommy Nettleton, and there isn't a day that goes by, I don't ask myself why! We all paid a terrible price for this thing called honor and freedom. You go into combat with a weapon and by the grace of God make it out alive, but carry a strange sense of guilt within you the rest of your life. It eats at you from deep within your soul; and if you let it, it will destroy you. It almost destroyed me!

My four years in the active duty Marines I loved, and a lot of people have said to me, it is a shame that with your record, and your love for the Corps, you didn't stay in. No . . . if I had only been able to be a husband, father, and grandfather for only four years, that would have been a shame!

Yes, I left my beloved Marine Corps, but my beloved Marine Corps has never left me!

In 1984, I took up woodworking as a hobby and have been doing it ever since. It became a labor of love and continues to be to this day. It became one of the vices that helped me through those difficult days.

I still try to play golf, but only on occasions; I continue to remain passionate on the golf course because of my conversation with God, years ago; when I am out there all alone, and if I listen very carefully I can hear Him say, forgive yourself; and again I say, I will try, Lord, I will surely try!

One of my happiest times is when all of my children and grandchildren are all with me. I love having them around me. It is these times when the Pretty Lady and I are most content. Although it doesn't happen as often as it used to, Lori and her family have moved to Alabama, and the others have moved only a comfortable distance away; however work and commitments keep their visits to a minimum, but we enjoy them when we can.

I have written this memoir to say this to my children and grandchildren, and to all young people everywhere; you can be anything you want to be, if you remain true to yourself (I can do all things through Christ, which strengthens me; Phil 4:13); put God first in your life and he will see you through anything. Be passionate about your goals and dreams; if you can dream it, you can achieve it! Always stay true to and love your parents; they have worked hard and sacrificed for you more than you will ever know!

Always admit your mistakes; you are not perfect! Anyone who does not own up to his/her shortcomings never learns from them; to put it another way, "Doing the same thing over and over again, expecting a different outcome (definition of insanity)."

Always finish what you start, in a timely manner (don't procrastinate). This is a habit that is very hard to overcome and will rob you of your goals and dreams; if you have this habit, get rid of it; if you don't, never start. I pass on to you what my mother told me: once a task is begun; never leave it 'til it's done. Be it large or be it small; do it well or not at all. Be dedicated in what you pursue in life; without dedication, there is no passion; without passion, there is only mediocrity; when there is only mediocrity, there is no purpose; and where there is no purpose, there is no dedication. Finally, never have self-pity; you lose your—self-worth and your self-respect. Life is certainly not easy, and a good amount of time, certainly not fair. There are many lessons to be learned from life, though. We may not learn them all, but retaining what we learn is one of the keys to happiness and success.

I have been asked the question many times: "Knowing what you know now, what would you change about your life, if you could live it over?" I have always answered that question the same. "I would change nothing about my life." I am very proud of my heritage, and the friends I have and the acquaintances, along the way. I am extremely proud to have served my country in peace time and in war (oh, by the way, no one has to thank me for it. It is always an honor to serve the people of this great nation, and if still able, I would serve again). I have no regrets and offer no apologies for any part of my life. When I lost my friends, Hatfield and Nettleton, a part of me died with them. Freedom does not come free. A price must be paid, and the price is always high. I paid a part of that price just like every other veteran. From the time we are born we are destined to die. We are born by the labor of our mother, but when we leave this world we must do it alone. The choices we make between life and death are our destiny. So never feel sorry for yourself. "I have never seen a wild thing feel sorry for itself; a small bird will freeze to death on a tree branch, and fall to the ground, without ever feeling sorry for itself."

In closing this writing, it is only fitting that I close on the subject of the game of golf; since it was many years ago, on a golf course, that I re-found my faith: "If you give up on this game, you give up on life. Never give up on anything. If you give up once, it is easier to give up the second, the third, and the fourth, etc. Giving up on something means you give up on you, so stay focused on life, accomplish the mission and, above all, never give up!"

Semper Fi

Edwards Brothers, Inc.
Thorofare, NJ USA
November 21, 2011